R. J. MERC

CAUSEWAYED
ENCLOSURES

SHIRE ARCHAEOLOGY

Cover photograph
Windmill Hill causewayed enclosure, Wiltshire.
(Photograph: J. E. Hancock.)

British Library Cataloguing in Publication Data:
Mercer, R. J. (Roger James), *1944* —.
Causewayed enclosures. — (Shire archaeology; 61).
1. Great Britain. Stone Age enclosures
I. Title.
936.2.
ISBN 0-7478-0064-2.

Published by
SHIRE PUBLICATIONS LTD
Cromwell House, Church Street, Princes Risborough,
Buckinghamshire HP17 9AJ, UK.

Series Editor: James Dyer.

ISBN 0 7478 0064 2

First published 1990.

Printed in Great Britain by
C. I. Thomas & Sons (Haverfordwest) Ltd,
Press Buildings, Merlins Bridge, Haverfordwest, Dyfed SA61 1XF.

Contents

List of illustrations

All dates are given in uncalibrated radiocarbon years and are thus signified by a lower case bc.

1
Introduction

In their simplest form causewayed enclosures consist of one or more roughly concentric rings or spirals of ditches, frequently broken by causeways of undug soil, and with the excavated material piled inside to create a low bank. Causewayed enclosures are probably among the least spectacular ancient monuments known today within the British landscape. Of the sixty or so examples so far recognised by archaeologists in Britain, some have been totally or nearly destroyed, many are visible only under appropriate conditions (usually from the air), while only ten can be readily appreciated on the ground. Why, then, has so much effort been expended, particularly since the mid 1970s, in their exploration and explanation?

The answer is that, scarce as they are, they comprise the earliest known enclosures in Britain, being built largely between 3000 and 2500 bc. Under excavation they have yielded the richest suite of data relating to the earliest societies to carry out animal and crop husbandry in the British Isles, offering a rare direct link with the origin of the present life-style in Britain. Unlike other monuments relating to this earliest farming (or neolithic) period, they provide a bewildering range of evidence, reflecting, seemingly, every aspect of the lives of the people who constructed them. Indeed the 'information explosion' that they have produced led in the 1980s to the complete reassessment of the social and economic environment within which these people lived.

This is, perhaps, not to tell the whole truth. To some extent the attraction exerted by these extraordinary monuments lies in the very intractability of some of the challenges that they offer. The societies that built them are entities for which we are not justified in making any assumption, however basic or simple. We have no contemporary accounts of their nature. We do not know, and almost certainly never will know, what language was spoken and it is only with the greatest difficulty, using conceptual frameworks at present in their infancy, that we can hope to reconstruct any detailed picture of the social and intellectual environment in which they functioned.

These challenges are made more daunting by the appalling attrition that has affected many of these sites, in the form of natural erosion or of subsequent human activity, during the five thousand years since their construction. Whether it be in the fenland setting at Etton near Peterborough or on a limestone scarp at Crickley Hill near Cheltenham, only consistent excellence in fieldwork, applied often over many years, will retrieve the full information that these sites have to offer.

The objective of this book is to present a necessarily partial view of the 'state of the art' in causewayed enclosure studies in Britain today. We shall consider four topics: first, the nature of these sites and the reasons that may have led to their development; second, the cultural back-cloth against which they are to be set; third, the history of their investigation and a survey of the different aspects of neolithic life that the study of these sites has helped to illuminate, indicating the variety of functions that the enclosures may have served; and finally, the legacy these enclosures may have passed on to later architectural tradition.

This survey will not be complete: the writer will select those aspects which will suffice to illustrate the variety, complexity and vitality of the picture that is emerging. In doing so he will necessarily draw upon the work and thought of many colleagues and friends which, in the outcome, he hopes they will not feel has been misrepresented.

2
Background

Why enclosure?

The first act of human enclosure in any landscape is a statement as important in that context as the first hesitant steps of Neil Armstrong and Edwin Aldrin in the greater conceptual universe of our own time. It is the first concrete expression of human will to control and exploit selectively our environment. It triggers processes of social, intellectual, economic and environmental development that are far-reaching, cumulative and usually irreversible. Today we could not conceive of living without the act of enclosure, which lies at the root of our social and intellectual organisation. We spend all day, every day, moving from one enclosure to another, often within hierarchical systems of enclosure. So fundamental is the concept to our way of life that it is difficult for us to conceive the importance and impact of it as an innovation upon those inside and outside the system that it represented. It is, however, necessary to make this leap of imagination before we can appreciate that impact, and it is perhaps one of the wider justifications of this study that it should compel us to make that leap.

Some six thousand years ago the first farming activities occurred among the mixed deciduous woodland of Britain and in the clearings at its limits. Pigs, formerly wild creatures of the woodland, were now encouraged to seek pannage in enhanced numbers, thus commencing the long process of attrition against the natural environment that has continued more or less unabated ever since. Cattle grazed the forest floor, where the natural canopy was sparse enough to allow grass and other plants to grow, and would have congregated in the flood plains of the uncanalised rivers. Severe damage would have been done to the woodland edge, but the constant trampling by hundreds of hooves and the fall of tons of manure would have helped to create a new kind of landscape — a fine turf supporting rich grass nurtured by perhaps a higher rainfall in southern England than at the present day. As well as supplying sustenance for animals, the woodland must have produced nuts and berries, fuel and timber for building houses.

Possibly somewhat after this first land-taking, containers bearing the seeds of wheat and barley would have been brought by sea from the continent of Europe. Land would have had to be broken and tilled, probably in the grazings created by cattle and pigs, and the seeds planted. It was presumably only at this point that the farmers' lives became radically different from those of the hunters whom they must have encountered, and from whom they may well have originated, also living on the forest limits and moving along the river margins. These hunters had for many generations taken the wild animals of the forest: aurochs, red and roe deer, and pig. Their skills would have been complementary and individuals and communities probably crossed the boundary between hunting and stock-rearing in both directions and repeatedly.

Into this highly mobile environment, however, an element of stability was now introduced: the arable field. With it came conflict of interest and the desire for control. In regions of more difficult soils and where turf was well established the initial breaking of the field and its continued cultivation demanded the introduction of oxen, castrated cattle, whose relative docility and enhanced strength enabled the use of the ard or primitive plough.

By 3200 bc trackways of timber were being constructed to allow passage on foot across the Somerset fens to the islands that lie in their midst. Preserved deep in the peat, associated timbers have revealed that the trees from which they were cut had been *pollarded* (the management of timber to foster the repeated production of poles of a required straightness and girth).

Grazing farm animals, wild animals, arable fields, managed woodland and somewhere to live safely and comfortably were all conflicting and incompatible requirements within this restricted landscape range, and the phenomenon of enclosure was created as a result of this conflict. Fences, walls and ditches must have become increasingly a feature of this multi-purpose landscape, their construction requiring and stimulating the production, in vast numbers, of digging and carpentry tools in the stone quarries and flint mines that became operative at this time. The removal of large timbers and stones that were obstacles to cultivation provided a further impulse towards enclosure construction, and probably the strength of oxen was harnessed to that process.

The existence of fields and crops and the need for their protection intensified the process of sedentism. Communities began to grow in size and permanence, allowing the development of increased specialisation of roles and skills within their social structure. Increasing investment of those skills and of labour in the creation of this controlled and subdivided landscape, and the increasing conflicts of interest flowing therefrom, probably prompted the need for some measure of hierarchical control and systems of inheritance. If this is so then it is probably significant that the period sees the first recognised construction of great monuments which, as part of their function, appear to have acted as the receptacles for the bones of a selected number of people: the long barrows and chambered tombs under construction from *c*.3500 bc onwards.

Yet the constraints of this relatively simple and precarious farming economy would also have limited the size of such communities. For the successful breeding of both their livestock and themselves and in order to facilitate the exchange of materials and produce, for example the edge tools and pottery apparently distributed over great distances at this time, centres serving a series of more or less isolated communities may well have arisen. Such centres would themselves have become the focal points of the conflicts of interest inseparable from the mutual use by different communities for different purposes of limited landscape resources. If a differential success rate emerged between component communities of such a catchment area, then eventually an emergent dominant community might adopt a special role concerning the catchment centre.

The centre itself would probably have served a whole range of functions including exchange, negotiation and celebration. In order to facilitate these uses, the limits of the area would have to be defined and indeed protected from the encroachment of the various factors already indicated. The technology for such definition must already have been a well developed feature of the current economy. It is in terms of this model, at the culmination of this sequence of development, that I suggest we can perceive the origin of the earliest formal enclosure for communal activity in British prehistory — the causewayed enclosure — by a date at present set at *c*.3000 bc, probably after half a millennium of farming. These enclosures were to be constructed over a period of more than half a millennium and were to pass from current use, though not from memory, probably *c*.2500 bc.

Where do causewayed enclosures occur?

These earliest formal enclosures for communal activity present peculiar problems of location and investigation to the archaeologist. At least five thousand years old, they have been subjected to repeated erosion by human and natural processes. The site at Hambledon Hill in Dorset, for example, has experienced at least five separate episodes of cultivation since the date of its abandonment *c*.2600 bc, involving around 1500 seasons of ploughing and harvesting. The effect of such treatment has been catastrophic, totally levelling much of the site to the point where it is visible only to the trained archaeological eye. Even from the air, repeated inspection has been necessary to reconstruct the outline of the site and, even after many years of intensive work, it is likely that elements still remain to be discovered.

This picture is by no means atypical. Only on a tiny minority of sites does any bank structure survive and frequently the causewayed ditches survive only as slight undulations in the present-day surface, again appreciable only to the trained eye or from the air. Nor is cultivation the only peril to which these sites have been subjected. Apart from destruction in modern times by quarrying (Offham, East Sussex; Rybury, Wiltshire; Staines, Surrey; Maiden Bower, Bedfordshire) and by housing (Abingdon, Oxfordshire), their frequent siting in positions of strategic and geographical significance has rendered them liable to destruction or concealment by later reuse of the site in other circumstances. Hillforts, often constructed in the first millennium bc, have frequently obscured earlier causewayed enclosures, either partially (The Trundle, West Sussex; Hambledon hillfort enclosure, Dorset) or totally to the point where they are only incidentally recognised during excavation (Maiden Castle, Dorset; Hembury, Devon; Crickley Hill, Gloucestershire). Nature too has obscured sites. Francis Pryor was fortunately skilled enough to observe upon a single air photograph taken at the peak of the freakish drought conditions that were current in the summer of 1976 the very faint traces of a single circuit of an interrupted ditch at Etton, near Maxey in the Cambridgeshire fens. Nothing was visible on the ground surface and indeed the site lay sealed beneath nearly a metre of alluvial silt laid down over a period of three millennia since approximately 1000 bc. It is likely that many such sites will continue to remain unknown to us.

The geographical distribution of causewayed enclosures would, however, appear to be clearly defined. There was a radical increase in the number of known sites during the early 1970s as a result of aerial prospection. Unlike the sites that had formed the focus of attention up to that date, situated mainly on the uplands of southern England and recognisable on the ground, these new sites were mostly located on the aerially 'photogenic' river gravels of the south and east Midlands. The new sites were located as far north as Barholm and Uffington in the Welland valley of south Lincolnshire and Alrewas and Mavesyn Ridware in the Trent

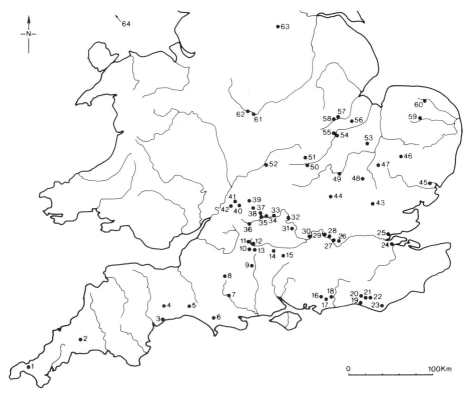

1. Map showing the distribution of known causewayed enclosures. Key: 1 Carn Brea; 2 Helman Tor; 3 High Peak; 4 Hembury; 5 Membury; 6 Maiden Castle; 7 Hambledon Hill; 8 Whitesheet Hill; 9 Robin Hood's Ball; 10 Rybury; 11 Windmill Hill; 12 Overton Hill; 13 Knap Hill; 14 Crofton; 15 Beacon Hill; 16 The Trundle; 17 Bury Hill; 18 Barkhale; 19 Whitehawk; 20 Court Hill; 21 Offham Hill; 22 Malling Hill; 23 Combe Hill; 24 Chalk; 25 Orsett; 26 East Bedfont; 27 Staines; 28 Eton Wick; 29 Dorney Reach; 30 Dunsden; 31 Blewburton Hill; 32 Abingdon; 33 Aston; 34 Broadwell; 35 Langford; 36 Down Ampney; 37 Eastleach; 38 Signet Hill; 39 Icomb Hill; 40 Southmoor; 41 Crickley Hill; 42 The Peak; 43 Sawbridgeworth; 44 Maiden Bower; 45 Freston; 46 Fornham All Saints; 47 Great Wilbraham; 48 Melbourn; 49 Cardington; 50 Briar Hill; 51 Dallington Heath; 52 Hampton Lucy; 53 Haddenham; 54 Tansor; 55 Southwick; 56 Etton; 57 Barholm; 58 Uffington; 59 Hainford; 60 Roughton; 61 Alrewas; 62 Mavesyn Ridware; 63 South Kirkby; 64 Donegore (Ireland).

valley in south Staffordshire, although possible sites have been identified at South Kirkby in West Yorkshire (10 km north-west of Doncaster) and at Duggleby Howe (8 km south-east of Malton in North Yorkshire), where a single ditched enclosure is set concentrically around the great neolithic circular burial mound which still stands to a height of 4 metres on the site. Other possible sites in the north can probably be discounted, as at Hasting Hill, County Durham, where limited excavation failed to produce confirmation of the site's neolithic date, whilst at Spot Dodd, 5 km south-east of Dunbar in Lothian, Scotland, a 7.7 ha enclosure comprising a pair of concentric interrupted ditches defined by aerial photography was shown to date to the iron age. Clearly, causewayed ditches are no guarantee of neolithic date and no convincingly neolithic causewayed enclosure has yet been located north of a line drawn from south Lincolnshire to south Staffordshire, or in Wales. As aerial survey programmes have been conducted in Wales, Scotland and northern England covering valleys rich in crop marks, it is likely that causewayed enclosures are indeed restricted to southern Britain. In addition, the slow-down in the discovery of new sites since 1980, despite the continuation of aerial reconnaissance, may indicate that a limit is being reached in the number of sites that can be recovered by this means. Nevertheless, new departures are occurring, as at Donegore in Ireland, where a causewayed enclosure of clearly neolithic date has been discovered.

   Why does this distributional restriction occur? Numerous changes in the cultural scene in the British earlier neolithic coincide with this broader division, and it may well transpire that monumental enclosure construction was a cultural feature restricted to the southern side of this divide. Roger Palmer has pointed out that in terms of maximum area there would appear to be a bimodal division of enclosures into those of 1-4 ha in extent and large sites ranging from 5.5-9.5 ha. The large sites comprised, even with the recently discovered addition of an eighth very large enclosure at Crofton near Swindon, Wiltshire, a heavy statistical weighting towards the upland sites of the southern chalklands (Windmill Hill, Wiltshire [9.6 ha]; Hambledon Hill, Dorset [main enclosure 7.55 ha]; The Trundle, West Sussex [7.07 ha]; Maiden Castle, Dorset [7.10 ha]; and Whitehawk, East Sussex [5.50 ha]). The lowland examples were Freston, Suffolk (8.55 ha), Fornham All Saints, Suffolk (8.04 ha), and the enclosure at Crofton (about 10 ha). An analysis of minimum area enclosed by any one ditch revealed a somewhat similar bimodal distribution with a group 0.5-3.0 ha in area and a lesser group of big enclosures between 5.00 and 7.5 ha in area, reflecting largely the 'maximum area' pattern; the Hambledon central causewayed enclosure was the largest of all single-circuit enclosures (7.55 ha) whilst the Hambledon hillfort enclosure and Maiden Castle retained the 'large size' preference in the upland series.

   Palmer's geographical analysis is the most valuable part of his contribution. On the basis of the morphological analysis that he

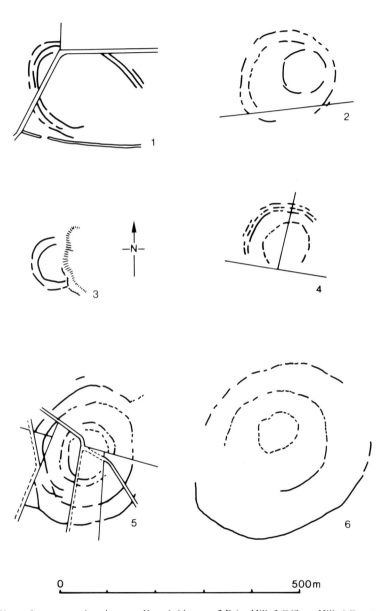

2. Plans of causewayed enclosures. Key: 1 Alrewas; 2 Briar Hill; 3 Offham Hill; 4 Orsett; 5 Whitehawk; 6 Windmill Hill.

had conducted, taking into account circuit numbers, narrow and wide ditch spacing, and maximum and minimum areas, he was able to perceive the possibility of four broadly defined regions within which the nature of enclosure construction was, on a number of counts, distinct. These regional divisions are fluid to the extent that different levels of analysis yield a varying pattern. Nevertheless they appear to reflect a fourfold division focusing upon south-west England (reaching as far north as Windmill Hill), Sussex, the Thames valley and the eastern Midlands, a distribution which becomes more striking when drawn in terms of the number of ditch circuits and their spacing. It is of considerable interest that this morphological analysis coincides strikingly with the analysis of regionally varying pottery styles.

3
The cultural background

What picture do we have of the societies that built these enclosures? We first recognise these early farmers as established communities by virtue of their material culture, which already shows some considerable distancing from that of communities on the other side of the English Channel. Furthermore, there are recognisable regional trends in the British material record that presumably indicate the establishment of discrete cultural (and possibly to some extent social) entities. These entities are best represented by the forms and decorations that distinguish the pottery of the period: this pottery takes the form of small cups and larger bowls and jars, round-based with generally fairly slack forms with sparing or no use of decoration. This general Plain Bowl Culture can be divided along regional lines into a series of styles.

In the south-west of England a pottery style occurs, sometimes called the *Hembury* or *South-western style*. It exhibits high carinations, large open dishes and deep jars of great potting accomplishment. These vessels are frequently adorned with a wide variety of lugs, both perforated and unperforated; a particular refinement restricted to this regional type is the tubular lug with flared openings, often called the 'trumpet lug'. These forms are totally dominant in Devon and Cornwall and to a large extent in Dorset, with a prominent occurrence in Wiltshire. Clearly defined centres for the production of pottery can be detected by the analysis of the grit content of pottery fabrics from the area. Two grit types occur, distributed very widely over the region: grits of gabbro rock, apparently located only in a limited area of the Lizard peninsula in Cornwall and presumably indicating the manufacture of pottery in that area, are found throughout the area dominated by the Hembury style and indeed further afield; similar grits of oolite limestone rock, and the fossil mollusc shells that form part of the make-up of that rock, enable us to recognise further manufacture somewhere in north-west Wiltshire or north-east Somerset between Bath and Frome. This oolitic ware is likewise distributed widely, although not apparently so widely as the gabbroic ware, reaching as far as Hambledon Hill in north-east Dorset.

On the east coast a further style of largely plain pottery is very widely dispersed from Caithness to Kent and has become known

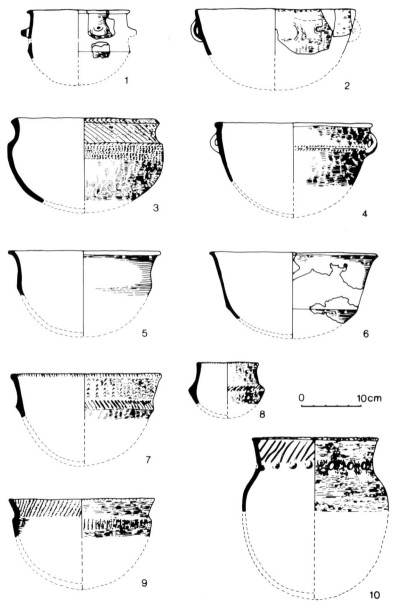

3. Pottery from causewayed enclosures. Key: 1, 2 Hembury style; 3, 4 Abingdon style; 5, 6 Grimston-Lyles Hill style; 7, 8 Whitehawk style; 9, 10 Ebbsfleet style.

as the *Grimston-Lyles Hill style*. The style is differentiated from that located in the south-west by the general lack of all forms of lug, perforated or otherwise, and by rims that carry a bead and flare strongly outwards. Both the Hembury and the Grimston-Lyles Hill styles appear to have been present in their respective regions from the point when recognisable farming communities occur. Both in Ireland and in East Anglia radiocarbon dating has suggested an early inception for the Grimston-Lyles Hill style:

Broome Heath, Ditchingham, Norfolk: 3474 ± 117 bc
Ballynagilly, County Tyrone, Ireland: 3795 ± 90 bc
3690 ± 90 bc
3675 ± 50 bc

With perhaps a more restricted sample of dates, the Hembury style would seem to be present from a rather later date, the earliest indications being from Hembury itself:

Hembury Fort, Devon: 3320 ± 150 bc
3240 ± 150 bc
3150 ± 150 bc

Between the Hembury style to the south-west and the Grimston-Lyles Hill style distribution to the north and north-east lies a central zone comprising central Wessex, the Cotswolds, Sussex, the Chilterns and the east Midlands through to East Anglia, within which area a range of decorated pottery styles co-existed, all influencing one another. These styles are members of the bowl-producing cultures current throughout Britain at this period, decoration not only differentiating them as a group of styles but allowing for more critical analysis of sub-styles than is possible in their plain counterparts, where form is the only criterion. These sub-styles are important to us as their distribution appears to reflect significantly upon the distribution of enclosures.

One of the more important of these sub-styles dominates the southern uplands of Sussex, spreading into Kent — the *Whitehawk style*, where the upper parts of the bowls were sometimes decorated with stabbed impressions arranged in horizontal or vertical linear forms or shallow fluted lines of incisions either horizontally or vertically stroked on to the pottery before firing. This pottery has come from a number of enclosure sites in Sussex in contexts that are near to primary as we understand them. One site in Sussex is, to a certain extent, exceptional — The Trundle, near Chichester. Here the assemblage displays only a few elements of the Whitehawk style of decoration and the preponderance of the vessels are plain (as in the Hembury and Grimston-Lyles Hill styles). Radiocarbon dates from the primary silt at The Trundle are earlier than dates from comparable material at Whitehawk, hinting at a development of the full Decorated Style in Sussex at the beginning of the third millennium bc, with perhaps a plainer style before this.

If it is reasonable to accept the possibility of a two-stage development of the Whitehawk style — the 'Trundle' stage and the developed 'Whitehawk' stage — then a third stratum of decorated pottery is visible on these Sussex sites, always in secondary contexts. This style is distinct from the apparently earlier Whitehawk style and has been named after a site at Ebbsfleet in Kent. The *Ebbsfleet style* comprised decoration on a number of pots (by no means all of the assemblage) covering the upper part of the vessels, including the occasional use of twisted or whipped cord impressions. This decorative style probably arrived on enclosure sites after *c.*2700 bc (at Windmill Hill, in north Wiltshire, the initial 'primary' deposits within the ditch yielded a radiocarbon date BM-74 2580 ± 150 bc). The style appears to be restricted in its distribution to the Thames estuary and Essex to the north and Kent and East Sussex in the south. However, it does not occur at the enclosure at Orsett, Essex, situated at the focus of its area of dominance.

The site at Orsett does, however, exhibit very close relationships with another pottery style of importance to us — the *Mildenhall style*, best exemplified in the large assemblage of vessels recovered at the site of Hurst Fen, Suffolk, excavated by Graham Clark, and closely related to a style of decoration found at the enclosure at Abingdon, Oxfordshire, often called the *Abingdon style*. We shall treat these two as one style — the *Abingdon/Mildenhall style*. This style dominates sites from East Anglia and the east Midlands to the Chilterns, the Thames valley, the Cotswolds and into northern Wessex, where it dominates the assemblage at Windmill Hill itself. The style comprised simple bowls and cups with relatively little use of carination and with decoration both on the rim and on the upper half of the vessel, often executed with cord impression or with impressed stabs or fluted strokes. Decoration was less prevalent at Abingdon than at Hurst Fen but the fundamental inventory of features was similar. There are unfortunately no radiocarbon dates from the site at Hurst Fen but a radiocarbon date from bone collagen at Abingdon suggests that *c.*2800-2500 bc is probably acceptable for this site. Nevertheless this site, together with the chronological evidence from Orsett and Windmill Hill, might suggest a currency for these forms from the beginning of the third millennium bc until the middle centuries of that millennium.

The pottery traditions that we have examined very briefly on the basis of the tiny sample available to us clearly indicate very broad regional styles that allow us to hint at supra-regional, and indeed intra-regional, linkages.

In summary, the cultural background teaches us to observe the widely variable natural environment of southern Britain against which communities of broadly similar background began to farm. Subtle and indeed more positive variations within the nature of that economy were inevitable, leading to variations of cultural adaptation, expressed in the surviving archaeological record as variations in ceramic decoration and form. Such variations are minimal in terms of the long time span and many thousands of square kilometres involved in this consideration. Nevertheless, in terms of pottery production (the most sensitive indicator to survive) four distinct groupings emerge: a south-west group, including Cornwall, Devon, Dorset, the south-west part of Wessex and up into the Cotswolds; a Sussex group; and a central group in the Thames valley, the Chilterns, East Anglia and the east and central Midlands, which is divisible into two distinct units — a Thames valley group and an east Midland group. To the north, north-west and north-east an ill defined tradition of independent status survives: the Grimston-Lyles Hill Group. As we have seen, this fourfold differentiation is partly reflected in the distribution and analysis of enclosures of this date in southern England.

4
Historical survey of causewayed enclosure studies

'A small Roman camp above Alton in Wiltshire' — thus did John Aubrey, writing in the 1680s, make the earliest reference to the standing earthwork remains of a neolithic enclosure, that at Knap Hill, Wiltshire. Appropriately, it was also to this site that the first excavational investigations of such a site were to be attracted, drawn by the very striking situation of the enclosure and by the quality of its surviving upstanding rampart. The site at Knap Hill thus has a dual claim to stand at the head of neolithic enclosure studies.

10 km to the north lies the enclosure of Windmill Hill, Wiltshire, set on a low rise, 2 km north-west of Avebury. William Stukeley came to this area in 1719. He visited Windmill Hill, describing it as a 'pretty round apex, the turf as soft as velvet. There is the sign of a very old camp cast up one half of it but unfinished.' He was able to perceive only the outermost circuit of bank on the site and the recognition of the two inner circuits had to await the fortunate visit by another great English field archaeo-logist, O. G. S. Crawford, on a morning of low sunlight in 1924. Stukeley had, however, in his remark about the 'unfinished' nature of the site, identified for the first time the causewayed or interrupted nature of the ditch.

In his perambulation of Windmill Hill in the early nineteenth century, Sir Richard Colt Hoare, the patron of William Cunnington, one of the greatest of the early barrow excavators of southern England, recorded that the site was depleted by ploughing and barely visible. Colt Hoare was also the first field archaeologist to record recognition of the hilltop enclosure on Whitesheet Hill near Mere in Wiltshire, as well as the enclosure set upon a low eminence 4.5 km north-west of Stonehenge at Robin Hood's Ball, where he again made special reference to the low state of the earthworks.

In 1872 Charles Warne, writing of Hambledon Hill, Dorset, was to record: '...yet how high soever the antiquity of the Camp may be, the hill on which it is situated has its turf impressed with vestiges of still earlier occupation, consisting of low, time-worn banks dispersed over its south-east side, and on the part overlooking Shroton, the trace of an ancient British location....' These views were echoed by Heywood Sumner when working on the site compiling his beautiful plans in 1910: 'The down outside the south-eastern defences of Hambledon Hill Camp has been dinted with modern diggings for flints, and thus it is impossible to form an opinion as to what sort of habitation existed here to account for these outlying banks and ditches. But we may be fairly sure that this simple multiplication of low banks and shallow ditches belongs to a different period to that of the great earthworks, so cunningly planned, that encircle and defend the approach of the Camp on Hambledon Hill.'

During the first decade and a half of the twentieth century there was a massive increase in the attention devoted by archaeologists and antiquarians to prehistoric earthworks. An important general account of British earthworks by A. Hadrian Allcroft was published in 1908 (*Earthwork of England*). Allcroft conducted his major fieldwork in Sussex and it was in this volume that the causewayed enclosures at Whitehawk and the Combe Hill first receive published archaeological attention and furthermore are classed together by Allcroft as 'small camps...where the vallum and outer ditch have but the slightest relief'.

In 1908 and 1909 B. H. Cunnington and his wife, Maude, opened some trenches to investigate the nature of the 'camp' at Knap Hill in north Wiltshire. The investigation was not on a large scale but allowed a number of important observations. Mrs Cunnington noted first 'the discovery of a remarkable feature which appears not to have been observed before in prehistoric fortifications in Britain.... It was found that the ditch, instead of being continuous, is cut into short and irregular sections divided by portions of unexcavated ground forming, apparently, gangways or causeways leading into the camp.' The recognition of this specific quarry-ditch technique was accompanied by further very important detail. 'The pottery is of the rudest description, freely mixed with large grains of flint, badly baked, hand-made, soft and friable. It was found associated with patches of flint chips in the ditch, showing that the people who used this pottery also used flint for their tools and weapons, if indeed they were not actually in the neolithic stage of their culture.'

In the summer of 1924 a remarkable series of aerial photographs was taken of archaeological sites in Wessex by O. G. S. Crawford and Alexander Keiller. These photographs, published in 1928, provide one of the foundations upon which future study of causewayed enclosures was to be based. The volume includes a magnificent photograph of the enclosure at Hambledon Hill. Gardner in his account of the hill states that 'two long barrows and some flint flakes point to neolithic man as being the first of many who have left their traces on the hilltop: indeed he may have built the earthwork now to be described, although this cannot be stated with any certainty in the absence of relics.'

By 1924 a stage had been reached when much useful information was available in dispersed and undigested form. Once these diverse strands of information became linked in the minds of archaeologists a new class of monument was revealed for study and subsequent progress was rapid.

Since 1910 the Reverend H. G. O. Kendall, rector of the parish of Winterbourne Bassett, had indulged his hobby of collecting flint implements on the flanks of Windmill Hill in northern Wiltshire and recognised the much denuded traces of the single enclosure noted by Stukeley and by Colt Hoare. In 1922 he commenced a series of very small-scale excavations on the site. Little is known of these investigations but they drew the attention of O. G. S. Crawford, who by dint of the low winter sunshine prevailing at the time of his visit was able to point out for the first time the existence of two inner enclosure circuits, now familiar to all visitors to the site.

In 1925 Alexander Keiller began a major series of excavations on the site with a short season in that year and a series of longer seasons in the years 1926-9. After that date he developed a long project which included the investigation of the great monument of Avebury and was to last up to the eve of the Second World War. Keiller was never able to publish the outcome of this massive programme of excavation and this task fell to, and was brilliantly accomplished by, Dr I. F. Smith in 1965. It is perhaps fitting that we should leave any discussion of his results until later in our account, noting in the meantime the principal immediate effects of his work.

The nature of the causewayed enclosure became clear and its neolithic date was established beyond all doubt. Such was the wealth of pottery, flint, stone and bone artefacts retrieved from the ditches of the enclosure (or 'camp') that it was possible to discern a material assemblage which rapidly became recognised elsewhere and prompted the inclusion of this material within the term 'culture'. The 'Camp' Culture exhibiting Windmill Hill Class pottery was first mentioned in print (along with the term 'causeway' camp) by T. D. Kendrick and C. F. C. Hawkes in 1932, although the term 'Windmill Hill Culture' emerged only in 1954 as part of Stuart Piggott's magisterial treatment of this period in Britain.

In 1926 E. Thurlow Leeds, Keeper of the Ashmolean Museum, Oxford, observed the presence of quantities of similar prehistoric debris in a working gravel-pit on the north-east outskirts of Abingdon, Oxfordshire (SU 511983). His excavation in 1926 and 1927 revealed that pottery of broadly similar type to that at Windmill Hill, but with a higher proportion of developed rims and decoration and more recently denominated the 'Abingdon style' (see chapter 3), and abundant characteristic flintwork were associated with a segmented ditch. This ditch cut off a low promontory set between two converging streams looking out over the river Thames 1 km to the south, at a height of 60 metres OD and 7.7 metres above the river itself. Abingdon was to remain for nearly forty years the only example known of a valley-bottom enclosure of this date. It was the key to a lock that has only since the 1970s been turned by dint of the intensive aerial survey of southern river valleys.

The doyen of early neolithic enclosure studies was E. Cecil Curwen. An aerial photograph taken in 1925 of The Trundle hillfort near Goodwood racecourse, 6 km north-north-east of Chichester, West Sussex, revealed the existence of an earlier, largely concealed enclosure within the later well known iron age hillfort. By 1928 Curwen had commenced excavation upon the site, had proved its cultural association with Windmill Hill and had shown the site to have three, possibly four, circuits of ditches. The ditches were found to be the repositories for rich assemblages of neolithic refuse: cattle bone (with sheep, pig and dog occurring in lesser quantities); much charcoal, presumably indicating the availability nearby of mixed woodland including poplar, willow, hazel, ash and oak; and pottery in the general 'Windmill Hill' style, but again distinguished by minor idiosyncratic features, notably the application of 'platform' lugs. Stimulated by this result, Curwen was drawn to the enclosure of uncertain form, mentioned by Pitt-Rivers and by Hadrian Allcroft, at Whitehawk, 2 km to the north-east of Brighton (TQ 331048). Curwen completed a survey of the site in 1928 which in its finished form revealed four circuits of ditch and left little doubt as to the nature of the site. In January 1929 the Brighton and Hove Archaeo-logical Club carried out a very small excavation on the site that demonstrated incontrovertibly its neolithic date.

Importantly, both the Trundle and the Whitehawk excavations were published with commendable speed. Further work was to take place at Whitehawk in 1932 and 1933 and again, on a very large scale, in 1935 in response to extensive development of roads and the racecourse.

In 1930 Curwen published his important paper entitled 'Neolithic Camps'. In it he summarised his own work and that undertaken by his contemporaries. He identified further examples of neolithic enclosures on the basis of fieldwork — at Combe Hill (East Sussex), Robin Hood's Ball (Wiltshire), Rybury (Wiltshire), and Barkhale Down, Bignor (West Sussex) — although, curiously, he did not include Hambledon Hill. He suggested that Maiden Bower, 2.5 km north-west of Dunstable in Bedfordshire (SP 997224), on the basis of finds made by Worthington Smith during quarrying activity on the site between 1897 and 1899, was yet another site of this kind. He also suggested that two sections of concentrically arranged ditch on Overton Hill near Avebury, Wiltshire (SU 114684), related to a similar enclosure — a suggestion resuscitated by Palmer. On the basis of fieldwork alone it was inevitable that Curwen should have included a number of misidentifications: Buzbury, Dorset; Yarnbury, Wiltshire; Scratchbury, Wiltshire; Dinas near Llanidloes, Powys; and the Brown Catherhun, Angus, Tayside.

The vital step had, however, been taken. The disparate body of information accumulated over fifty years and more was ordered and a class of earthwork defined. Curwen went further, however, recognising broadly the linked pottery styles that united the sites and drawing upon the European literature to suggest parallels between the British sites with distinctive causewayed ditches and counterparts in western France and the Rhineland. He listed the characteristics of the British sites as he saw them:

1. 'The tendency for the ditches to be interrupted by frequent causeways at short intervals.'
2. 'The tendency to concentric lines of defence, separated by spaces of the natural ground level.'
3. 'In some cases the defences are deficient altogether where the hill falls away steeply.'
4. 'The ground plans of neolithic camps vary considerably but if one is more common than another, it is the oval, more or less unrelated to the contour of the ground. Other varieties include a simple promontory … various outlying earthworks or radial ditches. The number of parallel defences varies too from one to four and this seems to bear a general relation to the

steepness of the hill, though not constantly so.'
5. 'The situations of the camps are also varied; the
majority are on hills but low lying sites occur …
some may be situated on abrupt and prominent hills
and others on gentler eminences. One very curious
feature is that in some cases the builders seem to
have chosen a saddle between two slight eminences
…'

However, a far higher proportion of the sites known to Curwen
were upland sites than is the case now. Curwen was ambivalent in
his attitude to the 'causeways' separating the quarry pits of the
ditch as an adjunct to the function of the enclosure itself. He
observed that these causeways either corresponded with gaps in
the accompanying bank or did not. Where they did not he was
content to regard them as simply quarrying irregularities. Where
they did correspond with rampart gaps he tended to regard them
as entrances but 'it seems to betray the idea that may have been in
the mind of the builders of our British neolithic camps when, as at
the Trundle and Combe Hill, they left so many entrances through
the ramparts'. Curwen ended: 'The problem, however, is not
quite a simple one, and cannot be said to be finally settled.' How
right he was!

Curwen contented himself with the morphological definition of
the enclosure type, with establishing the existence of eleven
examples of the type in Britain and with drawing correctly
adduced parallels from the near continent of Europe in the form
of similar and contemporary enclosures from the Rhineland and
western France. He did not embark upon any discussion of the
function of these sites.

This decisive event in the development of neolithic enclosure
studies was followed by two further major discoveries, both of
them fortuitous by-products of extended campaigns of excavation
within iron age hillforts. In Devon, under the direction of Miss
Dorothy Liddell, the excavation of the mightily impressive promontory fort of the first millennium bc at Hembury began in 1930.
The site is set on a long steep-sided ridge at 290 metres OD,
jutting out into low-lying country to its immediate south. In her
first season Liddell encountered a single causewayed ditch enclosing approximately 0.9 ha of the promontory tip and largely
concealed by a later defensive line in the southern part of the site.
Within this area she located over a succession of five seasons
evidence for very considerable neolithic activity, what may be

interpreted as evidence of a house structure and a complex gateway leading into the site, and a further earthwork, of unknown extent to this day, but probably defending a much more substantial area of the promontory at this early date. The excavations at Hembury produced a very substantial assemblage of neolithic pottery which, while broadly similar to the Windmill Hill material, did represent a clearly expressed regional style which has been termed the 'Hembury' or 'south-western' style (see chapter 3). Liddell's work at Hembury was followed rapidly by publication so that a great deal of her information was available in this form when R. E. M. Wheeler began his great campaign of excavations at Maiden Castle near Dorchester, Dorset, in 1934. In his first season on the site (site A), during trenching of the western defences of the earliest iron age fortification, Wheeler located the totally concealed ditch and remnant bank of a neolithic enclosure of some 4.5 ha extent enclosing the eastern summit of the hill upon which Maiden Castle is set. A further stretch of this western ditch was excavated in 1937 while in 1935 and 1936 the probability of a total enclosure was indicated by the location of further segments of neolithic ditch on the eastern side of the summit, again sealed beneath later, iron age defences. Outside the apparent extent of the neolithic enclosure on its eastern side, retrieved in the process of non-random trenching over the late iron age eastern gateway complex, was a series of eight pits containing deposits of neolithic debris.

These discoveries were to some extent overshadowed, for Wheeler, by the location of the great 'bank barrow' which runs for 540 metres, almost the entire length of the hill, oversailing the ditch of the neolithic enclosure on its eastern side. Excavation of a restricted area at the eastern end of the bank barrow saw the revelation of part of the interior of the neolithic enclosure and a number of features were noted there.

Wheeler's results were compiled and written under circumstances which still excite the greatest admiration, at the beginning of the Second World War. Largely as a result of these pressures this incidental aspect of excavations at Maiden Castle received perhaps less attention than it merited in the excavation report and where information is included it is not always easy to interrelate one group of data to another. Nevertheless, the artefacts retrieved from the site are generously and superbly illustrated.

The advent of war in 1939 imposed a moratorium upon further work on these enclosures and the enthusiasm and the impetus of the 1920s and 1930s was not regained with the end of hostilities.

In 1951 Professor Stuart Piggott, working with Dr J. F. S. Stone, excavated two ditch sections within the enclosure on Whitesheet Hill (ST 802352) identified in 1807 by Colt Hoare and Cunnington as an 'ancient earthwork, of a circular form, and which, from the slightness of its *vallum*, appears to have been of high antiquity'. The site was 'rediscovered' from aerial photographs by Leslie Grinsell, who noted that a round barrow of apparently bronze age date had been constructed on top of the bank and ditch.

Piggott's and Stone's small-scale excavation successfully sought to demonstrate the neolithic date and interrupted nature of the ditch at Whitesheet. Nicholas Thomas undertook a further small-scale investigation at Robin Hood's Ball, about 4 km north-west of Stonehenge in Wiltshire (SU 102460), in the summer of 1956.

In 1954 the Cambridge University Press published Stuart Piggott's monumental examination of the neolithic period in Britain. With the exception of its relative chronology, devised before the effective availability of radiocarbon dating for the European neolithic and now recognised to be of far too short duration, this volume, reprinted in 1971, is still a vital foundation for any study of this period. With its publication the modern era of causewayed enclosure studies begins.

5
The function of causewayed enclosures

The function of a causewayed enclosure is neither simple nor unitary. The idea of 'school' as opposed to 'church', 'bank', 'stock exchange', 'law court', 'parliament', 'barracks', 'hospital' and 'home' as separate functional entities was undoubtedly unknown to the earliest farmers in Britain. In simpler societies something of all or most of these functions would probably have been fulfilled in any focal location and, whilst we reserve our ritual for certain specified places, this *reservation* of ritual would in all likelihood have appeared very strange to an early farming population.

To people living with risk and with its outcome, the 'touching of wood' would come as second nature: to them, the idea of 'ritual activity' as something specialised, indicating a specialised 'function' for a site, would probably have been a strange notion. All of life, from the limited risk of birth to the infinite risk of death, would have entailed the constant need for 'ritual' activity.

Whilst acknowledging that a specialised function may be attributed to some of these sites and that this specialised function would undoubtedly have been but one aspect of a continuum of conduct reaching into every recess of life, we can consider the complex function of causewayed enclosures under headings that, in themselves, are a statement of our own simplistic viewpoint.

The causewayed nature of the ditch in these enclosures may not relate primarily to function at all. We have seen that not all 'causewayed enclosures' are neolithic, and we shall see that not all neolithic ditched enclosures are causewayed in their construction, for example the rock-built enclosures in the granite-based uplands of south-west England. Moreover two sites have been discovered in West Sussex that are univallate ditched enclosures dug in chalk but which exhibit no causewayed construction: Court Hill, Singleton (SU 898138), and Bury Hill, Houghton (SU 015093).

Causewayed ditch construction probably originated as a quarrying technique that suited the social organisation and the technological infrastructure of labour at the time. The quarry was intended to furnish material for a bank or rampart which was of widely variable form. The economics of labour dictated that the quarry source should be as close as possible to the objective of the quarried material. The lineal disposition of the quarry along the front of the bank was therefore dictated, and thus was the causewayed ditch of the neolithic born.

Defence and settlement

That early farming populations dwelt in defined and organised settlements is now beyond doubt, although enclosed and defended settlement is a relatively late feature of farming society in Europe. It was, however, present in Britain by 3000 bc, as we have seen, and appears to be associated with a farming economy perhaps dominated by cattle herding. Cattle are a mobile source of wealth which require protection, demand exclusion from the settlement area and, in stimulating easily satisfied greed, feed the notion of intercommunal conflict. Enclosure, and perhaps defensive enclosure, is a natural response to these demands.

On the continent of Europe great enclosures exist that are perhaps best explained by the need for the containment of cattle in an emergency. The vast defensive enclosure (25 ha) on the Dolauer Heide 35 km north-west of Leipzig, East Germany, and on a lesser scale on the Derenburg (3 ha), 20 km south-west of Magdeburg, East Germany, offer examples of this type of defensive enclosure dated *c*.2700 bc.

In Britain even mightier enclosures exist. At Hambledon Hill in Dorset some 50 ha were enclosed within a partial circuit of defensive earthworks which, as at the Derenburg, cut off the routes of easy approach to the hilltop. This great outer defensive circuit at Hambledon may never have been completed. Nevertheless a magnificent circuit of timber-reinforced rampart was erected and, whatever its state of completeness, its existing first phase of defence was reconstructed on the southern flank of the site; later, towards the end of its life, it was reinforced by a double line of outer defences converting the original single line of defence into a trivallate system of in-depth defence. There were three great timber-lined gateways and between ten thousand and twenty thousand timbers were used to build the inner defensive line alone. The whole was constructed *c*.2700 bc.

It is difficult for us to conceive a motive other than the corralling and protection of very large numbers of animals (and the animal-bone record at Hambledon Hill shows that these were almost entirely cattle) for the construction of such a vast enclosure. Yet the total lack now or in the neolithic of any water supply on the hill within the defensive line militates against any idea of a siege economy. The enclosure was essentially a physical and psychological statement of power. It could certainly have been used as a refuge for cattle from hit-and-run raiding but could not have withstood any prolonged attack — the cattle would simply have died where they stood. Set within this great outer defensive circuit were two smaller enclosures, which will be discussed later.

Further south-west than Hambledon is the site of **Carn Brea**, just to the south-west of Redruth in Cornwall (SW 685407.) Here a small 1 ha enclosure is surrounded by a far greater defensive circuit enclosing nearly 6 ha. The site was long assumed to be a hillfort of a later period, but archaeological investigation has produced evidence only for a neolithic date. Within the enclosure, excavation and field survey revealed extensive traces of cultivation that also appear to be of neolithic date. Perhaps after the harvest, when leisure was available to contemplate raiding, cattle were driven within the enclosure both for their protection and for their manure. At Carn Brea the outer enclosure was heavily defended. A reinforced stone wall was protected on the line of easiest approach by a ditch dug down to, but not into, the bedrock, while complex gateways with long barbican-like reinforcements were erected. Here there are no causewayed ditches, unless interruption due to the obtrusion of a mass of bedrock is admitted as such. The emphasis, as with the 'causewayed enclosure', is on the rampart — the wall built of great boulders hauled in from the surrounding hillside, for which no quarry was necessary or possible. Where a ditch exists (only the eastern side of the site) the intention is for defensive augmentation.

Within this great enclosure at Carn Brea is the lesser eastern summit enclosure of approximately 1 ha mentioned before. This enclosure is again clearly defensive but here archaeological investigation has revealed within it substantial traces of settlement. The wall of this enclosure joins naturally insurmountable masses of bedrock to produce an unassailable defensive line. The wall is composed of massive granite boulders, many weighing in excess of 2 to 3 tonnes, and must have stood originally well over 2 metres high. Set within the wall are a number of terraces, partly man-made, upon which timber houses had been constructed — a settlement of 100 to 150 people, judging by the number of house sites and the prodigious task of wall construction. The people living within the enclosure between 3000 and 2700 bc led a life of considerable economic complexity. Besides farming, of which we know little, they apparently had a major interest in a local axe quarry known to exist in the Camborne area (Group XVI rock), the products of which were brought to Carn Brea in large numbers and worked and polished there. The outcome of this activity must have been lucrative as it enabled the group controlling this site to attract exchange items from a wide variety of sources. All pottery vessels appear to have been imported from a major manufactory sited somewhere on the south-east tip of the Lizard peninsula, at least 30 km away from Carn Brea. A variety of chert sources in east Devon and Dorset were used by these people, as were flint sources possibly even further east. Such powers of attraction and the likely concomitant control of resources (as well as the physical presence of the site itself) bespeak the existence of a considerable power base, and power provokes envy, fear and aggression. We can never know the precise sequence of events but there is little doubt that Carn Brea was attacked by a very large number of archers who assaulted the site on all sides: thousands of flint arrow-heads were left after the attack (eight hundred were recovered during excavation); the wall was apparently deliberately slighted; and evidence of burning is universal within the site. After this catastrophic episode the site was never reoccupied. How many died during this onslaught is unknown as bone did not survive at Carn Brea. Clearly a prosperous and complex way of life was brought to a sudden end

4. The collapsed stone rampart of the inner settlement enclosure at Carn Brea, near Redruth in Cornwall.

and the impact of the attack must have been overwhelming.
Carn Brea is not the only such site in Cornwall. Work carried
out in 1986 has shown that another boulder-wall-enclosed granite
hilltop, at **Helman Tor** near Bodmin (SX 068607), was another.
On the basis of an exploratory excavation, it too has revealed a
large number of terraces for occupation within a broadly similar-
sized enclosure designed in precisely the same way as Carn Brea.
Traces of an outer enclosure exist on the western side, apparently
somewhat smaller in size than the great outer enclosure at Carn
Brea. On the basis of a small excavated sample it appears that the
occupants of the Helman Tor enclosure had a close relationship
with their local axe quarry source near Terras Mill, St Austell
(Group XVII), although both sites were importing the occasional
axe from the Group I source located somewhere in the Mounts
Bay area off present-day Marazion. It seems that much of the
pottery on this site, as at Carn Brea, came from the Lizard and
that the site was in use between 2800 and 2400 bc. As at Carn
Brea the enclosure commands an enclave of fertile land close to
extensive upland grazings and to valley-bottom settings where
fowling and perhaps fishing could be practised. Like Carn Brea it
sits just 2 km aside from the main east-west route across
Cornwall, partly followed by the present day A30 to Bodmin and
thence to the Tamar.

Following this route further to the east brings one close to the
south of the great iron age fortress at **Hembury**, 5 km north-west
of Honiton in Devon (ST 112030). Dorothy Liddell embarked
upon the excavation of the iron age hillfort in 1930 and, by
chance, revealed a single stretch of causewayed ditch cutting off
the end of the Hembury promontory and enclosing an area of
about 1 ha. Liddell's inspection of the interior was limited but,
where undertaken, produced a massive concentration of pits and
structural features (producing grains of wheat and barley), including one apparently entire rectangular house plan. This house
appeared to be set beside a timber-lined roadway leading across a
wider causeway in the ditch. Substantial traces of burning were
present at all points encountered in the interior.

The ditch itself had apparently been allowed to silt up for a
time but on top of this accumulation of debris lies a mass of burnt
material — timber that having fallen into the ditch continued to
burn there ferociously transforming the natural greensand into
which the ditch is cut to a wine-coloured hue up to a height of 1
metre on the ditch side. Oak, hazel and ash form the constituent
elements of this burnt debris — elements that could be associated

with the remains of wattling strapped against an oak timber framework. This layer of charcoal was never less than 15 cm thick and sometimes approached 60 cm in thickness. Whole blocks of burnt oak charcoal were noted in the debris as well as masses of burnt stone.

This evidence of conflagration occurs in conjunction with at least 120 leaf-shaped arrow-heads, many partly calcined by burning. Many of the arrow-heads were located in the ditch flanking the entrance causeway. The collapse and disruption of the rampart at this stage comprises the great bulk of the ditch filling and unfortunately any remnant bank was scoured away in the iron age. In the top of the collapsed rubble in one ditch segment the ditch appears to have been re-cut, with the possible deliberate deposit of pottery and organic material — a feature occurring consistently elsewhere. The evidence from Hembury, looked at from the viewpoint of Carn Brea and other sites discussed below, points firmly towards a site used for intensive occupation which at a final stage of its existence was attacked by archers and deliberately, and very thoroughly, burnt.

Hembury was part of a much more ambitious enclosure system. At the northern extremity of the later hillfort a 2 metre deep flat-bottomed neolithic ditch running for 25 metres and turning, probably to cross the spur again 300 metres out from the main enclosure, was located by Liddell. This ditch, too, had been subjected to burning and the apparent disruption of its rampart.

Before its destruction Hembury, like Carn Brea, had been the focus of extended and complex lines of communication. Substantial quantities of gabbro-gritted pottery imported from south-west Cornwall occur on the site. Bere flint and chert from Dorset also occur, along with axes of the same groups represented at Carn Brea and Helman Tor (Groups XVI, XVII and IV) derived from rock sources between St Ives and Camborne in Cornwall. This site appears to be situated on the route of overland exchange that has its western termini at Carn Brea and Helman Tor. The exchange activity continued beyond Hembury away to the east.

Perhaps the closest parallel for the situation that Liddell uncovered at Hembury comes as a result of the large-scale and long-term investigation of the site at **Crickley Hill** near Cheltenham in Gloucestershire (SO 927161) conducted by Dr Philip Dixon. Unknown as a causewayed enclosure until 1971, the site has never been cultivated although quarrying on a massive scale has severely damaged its borders and the later occupation of the hilltop down to the Dark Ages has necessarily damaged the neolithic evidence on the site. Nevertheless Dr Dixon has been able to observe the details of a long and complex sequence on the site in which the neolithic component displays at least seven stages.

Crickley pulls together so many aspects of causewayed enclosure studies — ceremonial, 'commemorative', as well as settlement and defence — that it is difficult to include the site under any particular consideration. Nevertheless, the parallel with Hembury compels discussion at this juncture.

The site at the earliest stage of use in the neolithic (Dixon's phase 1a) consists of a tiny oval 'barrow', which has revealed no burial. The material for the barrow was obtained from quarry pits set to either side. The idea of a barrow without a burial need not cause surprise as the phenomenon is now well known in the British neolithic. Two long barrows near Avebury in north Wiltshire (South Street and Beckhampton Road), for example, betray a similar 'cenotaphic' purpose. Whatever the function of this mound (and the few huts that lay near it, later sealed by the phase 1bi rampart), it was dismantled and its quarry ditch completely back-filled to provide an unobstructed site for the construction of the first phase (1bi) of the causewayed enclosure. This initial enclosure phase comprised a single ditch circuit (which was to become the outer ditch of the site as it developed). The ditch of this initial enclosure was broad, shallow and flat-bottomed with at least three, but probably five, entrances aligned radially on the centre of the site. The material quarried from the ditch was used to construct a broad and very low bank to the rear, on which was erected a fence of no great height. It seems likely that at some stage this enclosure was subjected to arrow-shot and Crickley at its inception may thus be termed a defensive enclosure of some 10,500 square metres (about 1 ha).

The next stage (1bii) was the construction some 22 metres within the 1bi ditch of an inner counterpart. This ditch was more substantial than its earlier equivalent, being 2.5 metres deep and enclosing an area of some 8000 square metres. It was also intersected by a large number of causeways, many of them far too narrow to be thought of as means of access. At least three and probably four causeways were furnished with a gate and were complemented by a gap in the rampart. All these gates were aligned upon the pre-existing gates in the outer 1bi rampart.

The rampart created by the evacuation of this ditch would appear also to have a low broad bank with again a breastwork built on its rearward edge. During the constructional stage of this earthwork a change of plan took place which led to the immediate back-filling of a short stretch of ditch and the ramming down of the surface to create a 'missing' causeway necessary to link up with a pre-existing gate in the outer rampart.

Within this 1bii enclosure house structures almost certainly existed and indeed they may well have existed before this phase. It is, however, almost impossible to disentangle this earlier phase of construction from the ubiquitous structural traces of the succeeding phases. The gateways were furnished with timber-lined passages closed by double gates.

Associated with the structures of the interior and with the filling of these ditches are large quantities of flintwork produced from raw material that was imported from a distance of at least 50 km to the site. The pottery from these phases is identical to that from later developments in the neolithic on the site and is similar to that from the site at Abingdon, Oxfordshire, some 55 km to the east in the Thames valley.

Perhaps after the attack by arrow-shot associated with the outer rampart, this double enclosure appears to have been deliberately levelled with burning brushwood thrown into the ditch and promptly buried. Five phases of re-cutting in the upper part of this backfill occurred (phase 1ci-iii) over a prolonged interval: acts of 'commemoration' and revisitation.

After this interval of unknown length there was a phase (1d) of major refortification of the site with a single massive ditch with no causeways through the defence other than the two required to provide access to the interior. This ditch was dug only about 1 metre outside the inner ditch of the phase 1b complex and almost inevitably during its construction the workers broke through into the deliberate back-filling of the earlier inner ditch. When this occurred their reaction was curious, as careful walling was introduced to block up the breach into the earlier filling. It is as though the discovery had struck some unpleasant chord of memory, stimulating a reaction seeking avoidance and conceal-ment. Continuity is indeed a keynote here as entrances and interior roadways replicate the earlier arrangements on the site.

The body of material quarried from this, the most massive entrenchment on the site, was used again to construct a low (0.5 metre high) bank some 10 metres in width with a breastwork again on its rearward edge. This bank was constructed with a kind of casement technique, with transverse walls running at intervals through the body of the rampart — a procedure which may have induced an element of stability. It is a technique well known in the construction of the broadly contemporary chambered tombs in the Cotswolds.

The two entrances of this new enclosure lead from the timber-lined gate passage on to discernible fenced and cobbled road surfaces within the enclosure. Besides the roads rectangular houses were located, ranging in size from 5 by 2 metres to 10 by 5 metres. There seems little doubt that this phase, at least, comprises a defended settlement and yet again the complex nature of these sites is apparent. In the western sector of the 1 ha enclosure created by this earthwork and apparently at the end of the road leading from the southern of the two gates is an enigmatic structure the function of which is most easily termed 'ceremonial'. The structure comprises a stone-built platform of irregular form with uneven extensions to its northern and southern sides. 'Cairns' of stone intermingled with much 'midden debris' then accumulated on these extensions. The central part of the platform had been kept scrupulously clean, possibly by this means offering a pristine setting for the apparent focus of the structure, a rectangular slab-built 'sanctum' constructed on the western side of the platform. The approach to the platform along the road from the east was impeded by a gate which opened on to the platform itself, while outside the gate in the centre of the roadway was a tiny vertical slab. Philip Dixon's careful excavation has indicated, judging by the wear on the road surface, that all of the foot traffic passed around the left (southern) side of this little orthostat.

The original significance of all this is unknown, although it is clear that complex ceremonial activity took place here in a segregated area within an enclosure otherwise given over to settlement in a defended context. This 'shrine' formed the focus of prolonged activity after the enclosure and settlement were destroyed.

As at Carn Brea, the phase 1d fortification met what appears to have been a violent end. A massive concentration of leaf arrow-heads lies along the line of palisade with a concentration of over four hundred within the entrances. This enclosure seems to have been the target of intensive, and perhaps tactically marshalled, archery. It is perhaps significant that no further occupation appears to follow this devastating assault.

Even so, the 'shrine' appears to have remained the focus of commemorative or at least continued attention. The shrine itself had been burnt down but subsequently (period 1ei) a low long cairn supporting three roughly parallel rows of fencing was built,

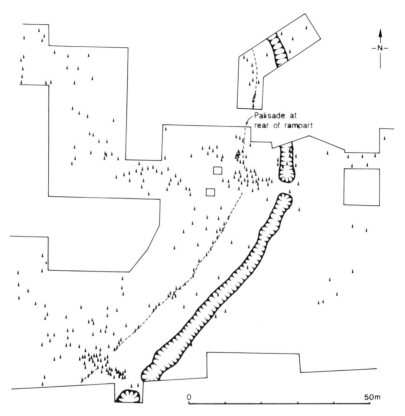

5. The distribution of arrow-heads after the assault on the final enclosure at Crickley Hill, Gloucestershire, as recorded by excavation. (After Dixon.)

burying the former track leading to the now ruined shrine. Later still (1eii) the shrine was incorporated within a low circular platform, which was in turn revamped, the central area being covered with a limestone slab upon which the further burning of animal bone took place. The cairn was also covered and extended to over 100 metres in length by a long mound; its sides had been marked out with slabs beneath which caches of butchered cattle bone were found. Analysis of the molluscs from the soil content of the mound suggests that the mound material may have been brought to the site from a wide range of differing soil environments, some of which occurred only at distances in excess of 2 km. There is a clear parallel, if at a smaller scale, between this

'terminal' Crickley mound and the long mound (or 'bank barrow') comprising the final neolithic activity at Maiden Castle, Dorset.
The juxtaposition of defence, settlement and ceremonial is also displayed at **Hambledon Hill**, 5 km north-west of Blandford Forum in Dorset (ST 849122). Hambledon Hill is a great trefoil-shaped chalk massif just to the west of Cranborne Chase in north-west Dorset. It is a wonderfully impressive landmark, visible for many miles, which commands both the principal route of the Stour valley and the great plain of the Vale of Blackmore. The crown of the hill at the hub of the clover-leaf outline was initially enclosed by a single causewayed ditch, surrounding an area of 9 ha, with subsidiary short lengths of ditch impeding access along the spurs of the clover leaf from south and east and, almost certainly originally, from the north. The precise nature of the activities conducted within this 'main' enclosure will be discussed later when the evidence for the ceremonial use of such sites is considered. Here we shall look at the evidence for defensive and settlement activity at Hambledon, albeit (as at Crickley) with a background of ceremonial activity.
At Hambledon any such consideration starts with a much smaller enclosure set at the tip of the south-east spur of the hill, known locally as the Stepleton Spur. The Stepleton enclosure is similar in size to Crickley, Carn Brea and Helman Tor (about 1 ha). It was almost totally excavated between 1977 and 1982 by the writer on behalf of English Heritage. Like Crickley, the enclosure has a long and complex history, beginning as a simple single-ditched enclosure of diminutive proportions. The ditch of this phase I enclosure was never more than 1.5 metres deep and its quarried material was used to create a rampart never more than 2 metres wide and encased within a timber framework, creating a vertical rearward and frontal face. This reconstruction is based upon the occasional traces of earthfast sockets for the vertical timbers of the rearward facade on the narrowly confined platform upon which the bank stood, and also on the nature of the filling of the ditch. We are thus dealing with a monument superficially similar to Crickley (both exhibit causewayed ditches) but which must, when in use, have had a radically different appearance.
The evidence from within the enclosure was, unlike Crickley, badly damaged by subsequent activity. Nevertheless, a large number of pits and fragmentary structural features were present but were not clear enough to indicate the form of the buildings. The pits contained what appeared to be domestic rubbish: broken flint tools, scraps of eroded pottery, fragmented animal bone and

carbonised vegetable matter. The last included emmer and einkorn wheat, six-row hulled barley and, uniquely in Britain, one seed of *Vitis vinifera* (domesticated grape), which may suggest the import to the site over long distances(?) of dried fruit. One of the features at Stepleton resembles an oven or kiln base, and debris from primary contexts in the ditch suggests the *in situ* working of flint and antler. A tiny skeleton of a still-born child thrust into a natural cavity in the side of the ditch could also indicate the proximity of domesticity and the warmth, shelter and nourishment that one hopes were associated with the hazards of childbirth. If a picture can be created of domestic activity on this phase I site, it is perhaps reinforced by the small number of objects of exotic origin found here in contrast to the contexts excavated in the main enclosure. Yet difficulties exist. The large animal-bone assemblage from the site suggests that its occupants ate well and wastefully — it might be appropriate to say they 'feasted' rather than 'ate'. Whole articulated joints of meat were partially consumed and then discarded, while less attractive parts of the animal were simply thrown away.

This is not a picture consistent with our current view of the diet prevalent among subsistence farming economies and may suggest (in conjunction with the evidence for imported food) that a high status group occupied this enclosure. This said, there is no conflict with the evidence from both Crickley and Carn Brea where the command of external resources, the massive efforts undertaken to provide defence and the evidence for controlled warfare might hint at competition between established hierarchies. The intimate association both at Hambledon and at Crickley Hill between hierarchical settlement and ceremonial complexes may suggest a sacerdotal rather than purely dynastic base for hierarchical distinction.

Whatever the case, the community at Stepleton eventually felt the need to enhance the defensive and monumental impact of its enclosure. The defensive scheme developed, as at Crickley, was not one designed to protect the settlement alone. It was designed to encompass the entire hilltop, enclosing an area, at least in its final stages, of some 50 ha — the largest neolithic defended enclosure in Europe (phase IIa).

Initially, a more massive and less frequently causewayed ditch was dug, enclosing on three sides the earlier Stepleton enclosure and totally removing the old phase I causewayed ditch on one side (the south-east). A gateway through the massive earthwork was constructed just outside the Stepleton enclosure to the west

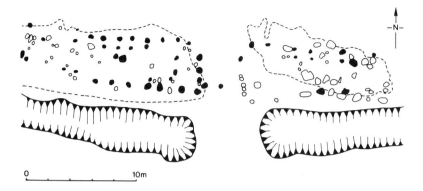

6. Plan of the post revetment of the box-frame rampart of the inner outwork at Hambledon Hill, Dorset.

and thence the earthwork continued some 800 metres to the western end of the southern spur of the hill. Here a further massive gateway was built before the earthwork turned north to run along the whole western flank of the hill. The rampart behind this new massive ditch was of 'box-rampart' type — revetted front and rear with substantial oak posts — with the front and rear revetment presumably tied together with horizontal tie-beams through the body of the rampart. Over ten thousand substantial oak timbers would have had to be obtained, transported, dressed and joint-worked to furnish the raw materials for this gigantic undertaking. This rampart was probably replaced once during its life and enlarged (phase IIb) to be wider and higher. During this process the occupation of the Stepleton enclosure continued and its occupation debris appears sporadically on the floor of the new phase II ditch, which was recut during the phase IIb reconstruction and subsequently cleaned out.

Later, yet further defensive measures appeared necessary and a massive reinforcement of the defensive system took place (phase III). On the southern flank of the hill (the most easily approached) two lines of lesser ditches were added to the exterior of the phase IIa/b rampart to create a massive trivallate defence with a smaller box rampart set within the inner ditch and a simple 'dump' bank, probably surmounted by a fence, set within the outer. Evidence of collapsed material from the bottom of the inner ditch suggests that both box ramparts were surmounted by a breastwork of hurdling mounted upon a timber framework.

That the threat which prompted this massive additional effort at Stepleton (itself requiring at least another ten thousand substantial timbers) was a critical one may be suggested by the carrying of the phase III ditches and ramparts right across the gateways of the earlier phase II construction. Whatever the cause, while the ditches of phase III were completely clean a catastrophic conflagration overwhelmed the entire complex, with evidence existing for the inner (phase IIa/b) rampart being on fire over a length of at least 120 metres. The fire raged in what appears to have been a strong north-westerly wind and ash and daub were blown on to the floor of the outer ditch.

The burning of the timberwork encasing the rampart led to the mass of chalk within the 'box' collapsing forward into the ditch, where it sealed some of the most revealing evidence relating to this destruction phase. Perfectly preserved beneath this collapse were two intact skeletons of robust young men aged about twenty. One had been shot by an arrow in the back while carrying a young child. He had then either been pitched (while still holding the child) or had fallen forward into the ditch-butt of one of the entrance causeways into the Stepleton enclosure. The arrow-head remained in his thoracic cavity and many of the bones remained where the child had been crushed or smothered beneath him. Two other skeletons, one of a young man and another of an older woman, lay imperfectly sealed by the rubble collapse and had been partly gnawed and dismembered by dogs and other scavengers after the site was deserted. One young man was buried in a pit grave in a crouched position with fragments of a pot and a quern-stone laid with him. His grave was back-packed with scorched chalk that was probably derived from the wrecked rampart debris. He may represent a casualty among the victorious assailants of the site, for whom there was time to arrange some perfunctory obsequies. The defeated defendants were clearly left to take their chance.

These macabre details add some colour to the notion of neolithic warfare witnessed at a number of sites in south-west England. This warfare, at least when it occurred at the end of the site's life at Hambledon (*c*.2600 bc), was not solely a matter of ceremonial display or bravado. Men, women and children were killed, apparently in numbers, and possibly among both the attackers and the defenders. These conflicts must have appeared serious enough to their participants, if only to prompt the extraordinary defensive measures undertaken at Hambledon and the other sites of this group.

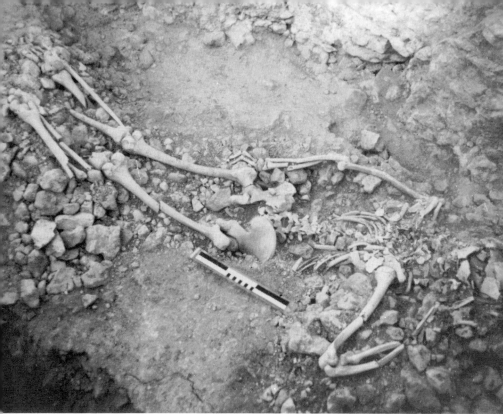

7. The skeleton of a robust young male, probably carrying a very young child, who was shot in the back and fell mortally wounded among the scorched rubble of the inner outwork rampart bounding the Stepleton enclosure at Hambledon Hill, Dorset.

One further question remains to be answered at Hambledon. Why did the occupants, and doubtless the substantial labour force upon which they could call, enclose the whole hilltop within this mighty rampart system? Either we have to postulate an enormous population seeking protection within the 60 ha enclosure, a population for which we have no evidence, or we must accept a more prosaic explanation. Tony Legge's study of the animal bone retrieved in large quantities from Hambledon has demonstrated that cattle were the most important species on the site within the economy of the occupants and their surrounding population. This is in accord with such evidence as exists from other causewayed enclosure sites. At Hambledon, Legge has shown that the balance of the sex and age ratio within the herd (as represented in the bone assemblage) indicates that meat consumption was based upon the residue of a herd principally exploited for their milk. Apart from being among the earliest well documented evidence for milk production in Europe (and where better than in the Vale of Blackmore), this information may help explain the vast enclosure and defended area on the hilltop. Large herds of cattle ranging over the meadow grazings of the Stour valley would have been vulnerable to rustling. Their protection would have been of paramount importance to the population who depended upon them (and the hierarchies who consumed them?) and thus the need arose for a great enclosure within which to drive them in the event of danger from marauding strangers.

Yet Hambledon has no water source and can never have had any water within the defensive *enceinte*. Thus cattle could have been kept there only for relatively short periods, two or three days at most. This may indicate the nature of warfare: deadly but short, more in the nature of raiding than the kind of warfare with which we are historically familiar. In these circumstances the enclosure at Hambledon could have sheltered many hundreds of cattle, suggesting the scale of the economic basis upon which the site was founded.

Discussion of the great enclosure at Hambledon prompts comparison with the 9 ha outer enclosure at Carn Brea and the outer earthworks revealed by Liddell at Hembury. However, the outworks at Hambledon were discovered only after intensive aerial photographic and ground survey. At Crickley Hill a second enclosure, The Peak, has been located by Tim Darvill, within 1 km of the former site. It appears to be yet another settlement with flint-working debris and evidence of sophisticated and multi-purpose pottery manufacture as well as, like Crickley, evidence for a cattle-dominated economy. Were these two sites, The Peak and Crickley, like those on Hambledon Hill, united within a greater conception now invisible on the surface? At the very least the juxtaposition of sites like Crickley and The Peak, both discovered since the mid 1970s, must prompt us to ask how many such sites remain for us to discover. At The Peak, in the very limited area of ditch excavated, a substantial number of leaf arrow-heads were located.

At Hambledon the Stepleton enclosure dominates the south-eastern spur 800 metres from the main enclosure, set at the focus of the hill. But what about the northern and most easily defended spur, now the site of the later prehistoric hillfort? Intensive fieldwork here revealed an early enclosure sealing off about 5 ha of the northern spur tip. Excavation located the ditch and rampart of this enclosure and showed the ditch to be irregularly hewn in the chalk to a depth slightly greater than causewayed ditches elsewhere on the hill. Unfortunately despite the excavation of over 5 metres of its length, not a single artefact or block of organic material was located. No artefacts that could be dated to before the iron age were found during the excavation, yet the iron age occupation on the site, in the form of a house platform, was set at a level created when the ditch in question had gradually silted to a point where it was scarcely recognisable on the surface.

It is thus impossible to argue for a third spur-tip enclosure at Hambledon, although it is difficult to see to what other period of activity the univallate spur-tip enclosure could belong and certainly the writer believes it to be neolithic. Should this be correct, then why was the site not occupied and attacked? Perhaps it was simply too exposed for comfort and left in abeyance after its construction.

Of other sites that produce evidence of settlement three deserve special mention, those at Orsett, Staines and Etton.

The site at **Orsett**, Essex (TQ 653806), 2 km east of Grays Thurrock, lies on a low gravel spur overlooking a watercourse 300 metres to the south which enters the river Thames 4.5 km away to the east. In situation, the monument is best paralleled by other sites in the Thames valley, such as Staines and Abingdon.

The site comprises an outer enclosure containing approximately 1.7 ha defined by two concentric and closely spaced causewayed ditches with, set upon the inner edge of the inner ditch, a continuous palisade. The excavators, J. Hedges and D. Buckley, were convinced that the material from the two ditches was piled as a turf-revetted rampart *between* the two ditches. Once again (remembering Crickley Hill and Hambledon) we see the enormous variety of original appearance that may be concealed by the common factor of causewayed ditch digging, the phenomenon that survives in the field record. Set within this enclosure (which it is difficult to view as other than defensive) is a further enclosure which could (judging by its eccentric conformation) relate to a different phase of site use. It comprises a single causewayed ditch enclosing an area of about 1 ha, defined by a ditch with a bank piled on the inner edge. The inner ditch reveals evidence of re-cutting that is also present on other sites (see below).

The entrance was approached by a roadway between the butts of the two concentric ditches. Within these two barriers (with their intervening rampart) stood a timber palisade with a gateway with gates possibly closing upon a central gatepost. Within these gates is a V-shaped setting which could be a stock-control mechanism for dividing animals upon entry. Unfortunately no bone survived to quantify this suggestion.

The site at **Staines**, Surrey (TQ 024726), lies in the Colne valley delta 1.6 km from the point where this river meets the Thames. It is set upon a slight spur within easy reach of water. The excavation of this site revealed a particularly substantial area of the interior; inside were found pits, post holes, fence lines, gullies and considerable quantities of burnt flint, all suggesting a long period of occupation. Once again the dominant animal species on the site was cattle, followed by sheep and pig, the bone in such a state of fragmentation as perhaps to suggest domestic activity. In its flood-plain setting it is possible that the Staines enclosure was accessible only during part of the year but the complex range of woodland, marshland and river-terrace areas close to the site offered a variety of habitats that must have been an attraction to semi-permanent or permanent occupation of the site. As with other enclosures where a 'settlement' or 'domestic' function can be inferred, the situation is complex: the segmented ditches were clearly the subject of re-cutting, a small number of human bone depositions and ditch-terminal concentrations of material. None of these things suggests normal domestic activity. Clearly, in the neolithic they were part of the range of activities that might be expected on a site where settlement *also* took place. To judge by the heavy preponderance of discarded neolithic material within the inner of the two concentric causewayed ditches on the site, this activity was focused in the central area. Possible house structures survive on the interior area with a clear 5 metres wide band within the inner ditch where its consorting bank once stood. If, as seems likely, the bank occupied the whole width of this band, and if all of its constituent material was derived from the ditch then it must have been very low.

This mystifying picture of mixed function, as much a hallmark of the conduct on causewayed enclosure sites as any other, is reflected equally at the site excavated by Francis Pryor at **Etton**, Maxey, near Peterborough (TF 138073). The site at Etton lies in a setting rather different from Orsett and very different from the high-relief sites like Hambledon and Crickley Hill. Pryor's extensive excavation of this important site, uniquely surviving in waterlogged conditions, has shown that occupation was only one among a complex series of functions.

Etton lies on the flood plain of the river Welland directly beside an ancient stream course. Fluvial and marine change over the past five millennia has covered the site in up to 0.75 metres of alluvium. This thick 'blanket' ensured that the site remained undiscovered until unusually dry conditions in 1976 revealed slight traces of the tell-tale causewayed ditch on an aerial

8. Wood, pottery sherds and animal bone including horn cores preserved within waterlogged conditions near the floor of the causewayed enclosure ditch at Etton, Maxey, Cambridgeshire — a remarkable glimpse at what presumably many such ditches would have originally looked like. (Photograph: Francis Pryor.)

photograph. Once it was discovered, the waterlogged condition of the site was found to have preserved many things which do not appear elsewhere. Once again, the soubriquet 'causewayed enclosure' covers an enormous variety in prehistoric terms. Here, the causewayed ditch was dug into gravel and the quarried product was spread on the interior to consolidate the surface and to fill hollows, apparently no attempt being made to create a bank or rampart of any kind. The ditch appears to have been open for only a relatively short period, perhaps seasonally, and has been re-cut up to eight times, possibly to act as a sump to keep the site interior dry underfoot or possibly for less mundane reasons.

Within the enclosure the trampled nature of the surface deposits and the presence of at least one rectangular structure would suggest that one function of the enclosure was settlement. Cereal pollens retrieved from the ditch sediments attest the arable component of the economy while the dominant bovine component of the bone assemblage matches the situation at other sites. The work by Miranda Armour Chelus and Juliet Clutton-Brock on the cattle bone from this site suggests that the very high rate of occurrence of osteo-arthritis among the animals was possibly due to stress caused by their use for traction. Certainly the use of traction for ard ploughing occurs in the earlier neolithic as far north as Shetland, dated before 2500 bc, and in the south, where ard marks in the underlying bedrock are known sealed beneath long barrows of the period.

So far, then, the scene is of a homestead or paddock set within an arable enclave in a largely open grassland landscape in which cattle could seasonally graze. However, the deposits in the ditch once again show the intermingling of everyday life and ritual in the neolithic. In the butt of one of the ditch segments, deposits that make no sense as casual rubbish disposal were encountered. Small neatly piled bundles of butchered meat (now bone) occur as well as neatly bundled groups of calf bones and a complete pottery vessel of Mildenhall ware apparently set on a birch-bark mat. One sector of the ditch at Etton appears to have been deliberately back-filled with gravel, carefully placed, and deposits set both within and below the back-filling. In one instance cremated human bone was placed next to a human skull accompanied by an antler 'baton' and a small standing stone set up over a smashed pottery vessel. A wooden vessel was placed nearby. The suggestion must be that some non-domestic urge was satisfied by these tokens of gratitude, submission or propitiation placed within a water-filled ditch at the limit of the settlement area.

One other surprise occurred at Etton: the discovery on the opposite bank of the extinct stream bed from the Etton enclosure of another partially enclosed settlement of similar date (Etton Woodgate I). The Etton Woodgate site is not itself without parallels, the site excavated between 1954 and 1958 by Professor Graham Clark at Hurst Fen, Suffolk (TL 726768), being an obvious example.

Other sites of defensive location and stature and/or settlement function where excavation is either too slight or ill documented (or has not taken place) include the sites at Rybury and Knap Hill in north Wiltshire (SU 083640 and SU 122636 respectively).

Ceremonial function

Sites like Crickley Hill and Etton demonstrate the subtle interaction of 'settlement', defensive and ceremonial activity. This functional welding almost certainly reflects the reality of neolithic ways of life. Moreover, the lifespan, perhaps episodic, of many causewayed enclosures may well have exceeded five hundred years during which period there is a strong likelihood that more or less subtle changes in activity and function took place on any one site. Nevertheless there are a number of sites that suggest strongly that their primary role was ceremonial and indeed that certain specific areas were devoted to ceremonial and ritual activity.

Perhaps the site that offers the clearest perception of these processes is the main enclosure at **Hambledon Hill**. The story here, like that at Crickley, is a long and complex one, demonstrating an astounding continuity of tradition.

At a date probably before 2800 bc the main enclosure on the crown of Hambledon Hill was constructed. Once again, an uneven lobate causewayed ditch was excavated as a quarry to provide, in this instance, chalk rubble to fill what was possibly a timber-revetted 'packing case' rampart (phase I). One entrance to the enclosure was detected on the ridge of the eastern spur approaching the site, presumably closed off by a gate suspended from a substantial gatepost, of which clear traces were found. We do not know the primary function of this enclosure. Whatever initial deposits occurred in the ditch were almost totally cleaned out at nearly every point inspected. Experimental earthwork construction on chalk subsoils has shown that the initial material to accumulate on the floor of such a ditch is a thick deposit of chalk wash and humic material derived from the ditch sides and from the consequent collapse of turf. Such deposits rarely occur at Hambledon, suggesting that these deposits were deliberately removed — and along with them any cultural evidence of initial activity. That such initial deposits had at one time accumulated at Hambledon is demonstrated by the truncated remains of such deposits left *in situ* by the ditch cleaners in clefts in the ditch sides.

This prologue of ditch cleaning is difficult to explain. If the 'ditch' is, as we have suggested, largely a source for rampart material (the rampart style varying widely from site to site), then it presumably took on some greater significance with the passage of time. At Hambledon it was cleaned out before the secondary deposition (phase II) of a series of deposits which bespeak ceremonial deposition of defleshed or partly defleshed human bone. At various points on the ditch floor newly cleaned, deliberate and carefully disposed deposits of pottery, stone and flint implements and animal bone were located, with concentrations often occurring in ditch butts. These deposits were associated with frequently carefully placed collections of human skeletal

9. The irregular lobate form of the causewayed ditches at Hambledon Hill, Dorset. Note the very narrow causeway and the skull sitting upright on the floor of the ditch in the furthest segment.

Causewayed Enclosures

material. Often this takes the form of human skulls carefully 'set up' on the floor of the ditch. In one instance a skull so placed had been left for a long period so that silting penetrated the void of the braincase and became compacted there. Then someone entered the ditch and reversed the position of the skull, but they

10. Close-up of a skull on the floor of the outwork ditch at Hambledon Hill, Dorset.

could not reverse the direction of the compacted silting which was detected by archaeologists nearly five thousand years later. Even given the large amount of human bone in the secondary silts at Hambledon, the proportion of skulls and cranial fragments to post-cranial material is very high, suggesting the deliberate selection of the former for placement in the ditch. All the skulls lack their cognate lower mandibles and proximate vertebrae, suggesting that they were defleshed when placed in the ditch. The bulk of the remaining human skeletal debris comprises dis-articulated fragments but further groupings deserve special mention here. Two burials of children of about eight years old were inserted, flexed, in shallow declivities in the ditch floor, one burial furnished with bone beads which, when strung, comprised some kind of hair-tying mechanism. Both burials were covered with carefully built cairns of flint nodules. In addition, the whole central part of the cadaver of a young man of about fifteen years of age — the trunk and thighs — was found in articulated condition again on the cleaned floor of the ditch. This grisly mass had become detached in the course of decay from the thorax and the lower limbs, and the stubborn muscle mass had been dragged into the ditch by dogs, leaving traces of their gnawing on the bones.

These macabre details serve to illustrate the abundance of human skeletal and cadaveric material lying exposed within the confines of, and perhaps around, the main enclosure at Hamble-don Hill. Furthermore, these remains were at least in some instances freely accessible to dogs, and possibly to wolves.

This kind of evidence is so far unique in Britain and this degree of accessibility of large quantities of human skeletal material is consonant with the practice of excarnation — the exposure of human bodies to the elements to allow the decay of the fleshy parts. Such practices probably occurred in neolithic tombs from Wessex to the Orkneys. Human skeletal assemblages from these tombs suggest by their frequently fragmentary and incom-plete nature that bodies had been initially exposed elsewhere to decay before being bundled up and transported to the tomb, during which process losses of smaller bones often occurred.

It thus seems reasonable to suggest that in its initial phase of use the 9 ha main enclosure at Hambledon was a gigantic necropolis within which human bodies were exposed to the elements. The grisly sights and sounds to be associated with such a process need hardly be dwelt upon! Excavation of the interior could not be expected to produce vast quantities of human bone. Erosion, both natural and agricultural, over five millennia has removed about 0.5 metre of the original subsoil surface. Furthermore, experimental annual observation of freshly dead sheep in the Scottish uplands has shown that the remains of an animal newly dead in the spring are scarcely present by the following spring and not at all in the year beyond that.

Nevertheless a massive sample of 10 per cent of the interior of the main enclosure at Hambledon was examined, producing the eroded and damaged remains of 92 pits. A number of these pits had been dug and then apparently left open so that natural silt accumulated on their bottoms. This accumulation having taken place, objects were placed in the pits that in every instance appear to be exotic in the context of the site. Gabbro-gritted pottery, the distribution of which from the Lizard peninsula in Cornwall has already been discussed, occurs only within the pits of the main enclosure. Furthermore, in at least three instances complete vessels of gabbro ware, two of quite exceptional size and quality, had been placed in these pits. Also from Cornwall, some 300 km away, came stone axes of rock Groups IV, XVI and XVII, the same sources that occur in combination at Carn Brea (Cornwall), Hembury (Devon) and Maiden Castle (Dorset). As well as axe fragments, stone rubbers produced from a glauconite sandstone, which appears to have come from near Budleigh Salterton, Devon, occur and 24 of the pits have produced foreign stone objects of one kind or another. From even more distant sources, a nephrite axe and one of jadeite have been found in the plough soil at the main enclosure, almost certainly torn from the surface of pit fillings by the plough. Such axes probably have their origin in Brittany and possibly even further afield. The pits also produced quantities of red deer antler, otherwise very scarce in the context of the main enclosure.

Clearly these pits (in contrast to the pits in the Stepleton enclosure at Hambledon) were not receptacles for random domestic rubbish. They were the focus of careful deposition of objects which would appear to have been of prestigious value. These pits and their contents are probably associated with activity which, it is strongly suggested, took place within the enclosure — the excarnation of the dead.

It was probably not long before the enclosure began to fall into disrepair (phase III). The timber revetment of the rampart wall surrounding the site became unstable and with its weakening (or perhaps removal for other purposes) the massive body of sterile chalk dammed up within it flowed back into the ditch. At Hambledon there is no evidence for the deliberate back-filling of the ditch.

The site thus became a ruin although its significance within the surrounding community was certainly not forgotten. There began a process which involved the repeated re-cutting of the ditch silts and filling to allow the further insertion of deliberate deposits comprising an admixture of earlier material re-dug out and new feasting debris together with, apparently, human skeletal material.

The first evidence of this process at Hambledon (phase IV) is the digging of a series of steep-sided and very deep pits, penetrating almost to the original ditch floor, into the rubble collapse of the rampart. Into these pits were deposited the remains of what might be feasting together with a mass of black ashy material and skeletal debris. Radiocarbon dates from this phase range from 2720 ± 130 bc to 2530 ± 130 bc.

Following this phase of sporadic activity was a more complex and generalised phase of re-cutting (phase V). At this stage every segment of ditch inspected at Hambledon was re-cut over its whole length — a narrow trench no more than 0.5 metre wide and 0.3 metre deep — an act, seemingly, of re-definition of the whole enclosure. When this took place, silting and collapse must have already reduced the profile of ditch and bank to the merest surface undulation, and yet every (barely visible) causeway is respected by the re-cutting activity. Furthermore, it would appear that, in isolated locations at least, this re-cut was re-defined and

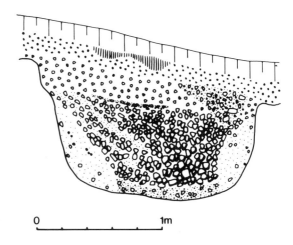

11. Section of a typical ditch at Hambledon Hill main enclosure, Dorset.

0   1m

dug out up to at least four times. Once again, within these re-cuts
(or at least within the latest of them) substantial deposits of
animal bone, pottery (some of it exhibiting the increased degree
of decoration that is associated with later manifestations of the
middle neolithic in southern Britain) and flintwork suggest 'feasting debris' with the apparently unavoidable accompaniment of
human skeletal debris.

By this stage at Hambledon the uppermost levels of the ditch
filling are within reach of the modern ploughshare and damage is
prodigious if patchy. Nevertheless, it appears that the top of this
multi-recut was jammed (phase VI) with a linear cairn of flint
nodules. The significance of this is unknown but it sits well
alongside those acts of 'termination' and 'commemoration' of
varying kinds that have been observed on numerous sites. It
bespeaks a society within which continuity of tradition and the
relaying of social ties was a paramount concern — a concern
natural to all farming societies with their inbuilt interest in land
tenure, genetic selection and calendrical notation.

The main enclosure at Hambledon thus appears to lie within a
continuum of activity with which long barrows and stone-built
chambered tombs in southern England have become associated
— the complex ceremonial, the 'rites of passage', associated with
death and the transference ritual that death brings in its wake. It
is therefore hardly surprising that some causewayed enclosures in
southern England (particularly hilltop examples like Hambledon,
Maiden Castle, Windmill Hill and Robin Hood's Ball) occupy a
nodal position with regard to known long-barrow distributions. It
was an additional bonus that Hambledon main enclosure lay
adjacent to two long barrows: one within the main enclosure
complex to the south and the other 500 metres to the north-west
on the northern spur of the hill. The northern long barrow, while
damaged in the past, is largely intact and still stands to a height of
4 metres for most of its 75 metres of length. The southern barrow,
however, had been badly damaged by cultivation in the early
1960s and its excavation was agreed by English Heritage.

Unfortunately the mound and any associated substructure had
been destroyed. The debris of its clearance, however, was still
available for inspection in the heads of its silted ditches. This
debris contained fragments of bone that could all be elements of
one adult male skeleton.

The ditches formed a U outline within which was set a
peculiarly 'Dorset' type of barrow, which it has been argued was
perhaps of a late type (*c*.2500 bc). The possibility of a single male

adult burial and the location during excavation of a Group I axe (a factory usually associated with later neolithic sites in Wessex) in the primary silts of the long-barrow ditch may well confirm this impression. Whatever the case, this barrow, when built, comprised a chalk mound corseted within a turf-stack revetment. Within a relatively short period it began to decay: the revetment collapsed and the chalk rubble from the mound flowed into the ditch. At this point the story (in the Hambledon context) invokes a sense of *déjà vu*. At this stage of decay the ditch is re-cut in exactly the same way as at the main enclosure itself. Furthermore, at the termination of this activity a linear flint cairn is jammed into the fill of the re-cut. Here would seem to be a replication of those acts of 'commemoration' and 'termination' that occurred on the causewayed enclosure and which surely must bind the barrow and the enclosure closely together within one continuum of ceremonial activity.

Ceremonial activity is notoriously difficult to interpret and so in the instance of Hambledon the interpretation has been dealt with in some detail. So far this cannot be done in such detail for any other site but in what follows it will be clear that such phenomena also occurred at other sites.

25 km south-west of Hambledon lies the causewayed enclosure excavated by Sir Mortimer Wheeler at **Maiden Castle**, just outside Dorchester (SY 669885). Located on the eastward route that brought the products of the south-west as far as Hambledon and beyond, this enclosure also has information to add to the picture of ceremonial activity already created. As at Hambledon, 'primary' deposits included human skulls (further examples of which were encountered in more recent work conducted by English Heritage). Deposits of burnt material, possibly reflecting the collapse of a burnt frontal rampart revetment, also occurred on the base of the ditch — burnt timbers that have produced radiocarbon dates of 3090 ± 60 and 3080 ± 40 bc, although human and animal bone from a similar context produced dates of 2910 ± 70 and 2690 ± 50 bc. Both Wheeler and Niall Sharples (directing the work for English Heritage) recorded secondary deposits of 'midden debris' in concentrations set into the top of the rapid rubble collapse of the rampart — deposits which are reminiscent of the re-cut filling at Hambledon.

Little investigation of the interior at Maiden Castle has taken place but Wheeler did excavate a fairly substantial area immediately to the east of the causewayed enclosure in order to explore the east gate of the latest iron age hillfort. In this area he located a series of seven pits, ranging from 0.5 to 1 metre in depth, containing what seem to have been specialised and possibly prestigious assemblages. One pit contained a carved chalk object of possibly anthropomorphic design, bowl pottery, an imported stone grain rubber and (certainly also imported) a scallop shell. Another contained pottery, red deer antler, two flint axes and a stone rubber. Once dug, several of the pits were clearly left open to silt, and some of the fillings appear to have been deposited in stages. In one instance at the base of the pit was a burnt layer containing a goat's horn, limpet shells and a hammer stone. Placed on top of this deposit was a further block of material including two dog skeletons and a neolithic bowl.

These deposits, and others like them, hark back to the pit fillings on the interior of the main enclosure at Hambledon. They are clearly not random domestic deposits and, as they lie immediately outside the causewayed enclosure, hint at additional complications to the function of such sites.

Further parallels to the activity at Hambledon were retrieved by Peter Drewett at the causewayed enclosure at **Offham Hill**, 10 km north-east of Brighton in East Sussex (TQ 399113). The site is set at the tip of an east-facing steep-sided spur overlooking the valley of the river Ouse. The site had been plough-damaged and comprised two concentric rings of causewayed ditch with apparently interrupted banks set within them, the inner enclosure covering an area of 0.25 ha and the outer some 0.5 ha. As at Hambledon, erosion had led to the reduction of the subsoil surface by some 0.75 metre; consequently the ditches were merely shallow depressions. Nonetheless, the tightly crouched burial of a young man of about twenty years was found in a declivity in the ditch floor, while six other human bone fragments were located elsewhere in the ditches. The pottery from the site resembles that from the enclosure at Whitehawk, 6 km to the south-west. Drewett has suggested that the evidence of feasting, combined with the relatively high proportion of human bone present on the site, indicates that Offham was an excarnation site as at Hambledon. Molluscan evidence from the site suggests that it was situated in a small clearing in woodland. Whatever the parallels with Hambledon, we must bear in mind that this site too probably originally presented a very different appearance. Little evidence for the nature of bank construction survives on the site but the suggestion is that it had several entrances in both circuits and was diminutive by comparison with the Dorset enclosure.

More comparable in size is the nearby site at **Whitehawk**, Brighton, East Sussex, excavated by Curwen in 1932 and 1933 (TQ 331048). The site is now much disfigured by Brighton (Kemp Town) racecourse. The site originally comprised four irregularly spaced rings set on a ridge rising slightly at its northern and southern ends. Like Hambledon main enclosure, the ditches of the outer circuit appear to be deficient on the eastern steep scarp slope. Again like Hambledon, there is the suggestion that the site may have been the focus of a more extensive earthwork system.

The site may have been constructed in two separate stages, as the filling pattern of the two inner ditches is distinct from that of the two outer ditches. The inner two circuits display very close parallels to the Hambledon sequence. Ditch cleaning preceded some placement of neolithic material on the ditch floor, followed by the massive collapse of chalk rubble from an unstable bank source. This material was then partly cut out to create a V-section gully in the ditch filling which Curwen referred to as 'the black triangle'. This gully was filled with a deposit rich in neolithic artefacts and included human skeletal debris. From Curwen's drawn sections it is apparent that the uppermost filling of the ditch has been truncated by more recent cultivation, removing any remaining rampart material. Nevertheless areas of 'enhanced protection' of the chalk subsoil survive to indicate the limits of the spread and decayed rampart and, set within this spread, Curwen located some post holes. This is all that might be expected to survive of earthfast revetment timbers and once again parallels the evidence at Hambledon. The second circuit of ditch was essentially similar in complexion to this. Within the inner enclosure, Curwen was able to excavate a substantial area, but to little avail. One pit was a grave containing a crouched inhumation of a man 'of middle age' associated with neolithic pottery and three mussel shells. Two pits were also located that suggested slow sterile silting succeeded by the deposition of selected prestigious materials that were found in pits of this kind at Maiden Castle and at Hambledon Hill.

The outer two circuits in their filling suggest a change of bank design, the bulk of the filling being a fine chalk wash material suggesting the existence of 'dump' type banks. On top of these deposits chutes of material containing organic matter were deposited from the inner and outer sides of the ditches. Within this material were located at least two female skeletons, one of 25-30 years of age and the other somewhat younger and associated with the bones of an infant. One of these skeletons showed evidence of disordering and displacement of bones, suggesting that the body had been exposed before its deposition in the partially silted ditch. The remains of five other individuals, three adults and two children, were located elsewhere in these upper layers. Given the volume of ditch material excavated at Whitehawk, the potential for human skeletal recovery on the site is in every way comparable with Hambledon Hill, if distinct in the precise ordering and formation of the site's development. Radiocarbon assays undertaken more recently on material recovered by Curwen from the primary silt of the outer two ditches at Whitehawk yielded two dates: 2750 ± 130 bc and 2695 ± 95 bc. The evidence at Whitehawk (and from The Trundle, 6 km north-north-east of Chichester, West Sussex; SU 877111) for cumulative construction suggests another recurrent factor in causewayed enclosure construction where multiple rings of defence exist. Orsett, Essex, also produced evidence of cumulative construction and similar evidence was found at Abingdon and Windmill Hill (see below). At Whitehawk (and The Trundle) there is a distinction between the patterns of decay and linked activity present in the inner circuits of ditch and those in the outer circuits. It would seem therefore that a further recurrent feature associated with these sites is their growth and alteration not only within great earthwork complexes as at Hambledon but within the context of single enclosures.

These points are exemplified by **Abingdon**, Oxfordshire (SU 511983), set in a very different location on a low spur in the Thames valley. Here two concentric causewayed ditches cut off the terminal slope of a promontory. The inner ditch encloses an area of about 1.3 ha while the outer circuit encloses some 4 ha. The site has largely been destroyed by quarrying and house construction but excavation over many years has allowed the reconstruction of a sequence of events on the site.

The primary structure at Abingdon would appear to have been the inner enclosure. The quarried material from the ditch was used to construct an inner bank, possibly crowned by a palisade with some material dumped on the outer edge of the ditch as well. The ditch profile indicates that it may have been cleared out on numerous occasions but, once major silting of the ditch commenced, re-cutting and the deposition of burnt organic debris occurred repeatedly. A radiocarbon assay from secondary infilling of these re-cuts yielded a date of 2960 ± 110 bc. Neolithic pottery, flintwork, animal bone and small quantities of human bone were located in these contexts. The existence of articulated bone groups within this material might suggest extravagant 'feasting' activity. Discrete basketfuls of midden debris also appear to have been dumped in the re-cutting.

The outer ditch was deeper than the inner ditch and a bank, possibly revetted with turf, was built on its inner side, while some of the quarried material may have been used to level the shallow remains of the original inner ditch. The nature of the filling of the outer ditch indicates a lesser degree of re-cutting in the earlier deposits and less occupation material in the upper deposits, suggesting that this later enclosure surrounded a settlement which extended over the levelled former inner ditch. While the primary enclosure at Abingdon presents some of the phenomena noted at Hambledon main enclosure and other sites, the second phase is probably related to settlement activity of the type noted at Hembury and Etton. Indeed, at Orsett the inner ditch similarly showed evidence of re-cutting while the more complex outer enclosure is more readily explained as a domestic site. These sites, then, may indicate changing use through time and reconstruction to cater for that change.

There are other examples of elaborate re-cutting and the deliberate arrangement of bone deposits within causewayed ditches. Ian Hodder has retrieved evidence of this practice at **Haddenham**, Cambridgeshire. Nicholas Thomas's section recording of his exploratory excavation at **Robin Hood's Ball**, Wiltshire (SU 102460), reveals clear evidence of a deliberate re-cut with dark organic filling, suggesting, as at Hambledon, that this is cut into unstable bank collapse that has accumulated upon a ditch floor that had been scrupulously cleaned. Stuart Piggott, excavating at **Whitesheet Hill**, 2 km north-north-west of Mere in Wiltshire (ST 802852), similarly documented a ditch section which had been cleared of all detritus before the massive collapse of an apparently unstable bank. After this collapse a period of slow silting ensued, into which, when the ditch was merely a slight depression in the ground surface, a steep-sided re-cut was dug into the underlying fill. Plain bowl pottery was recovered from the ditch floor, from the surface of the rampart collapse and from the bottom of the re-cut and, as at Hambledon, Piggott noted that above the re-cut was 'a layer of earth containing numerous flint nodules'.

Windmill Hill

The study of causewayed enclosures was originated by Alexander Keiller in the late 1920s at Windmill Hill just outside

Avebury in northern Wiltshire (SU 087715). Keiller began a major excavation on the site which ultimately led to the excavation of 370 metres of ditch in all three of its concentric circuits, and the examination of 1900 square metres of the interior of the innermost circuit.

To some extent Windmill Hill is exceptional in the degree to which it has survived as a visible earthwork today, particularly the substantial outer ditch circuit and its cognate bank which survives to a height of well over 1 metre. Unusually, this bank has preserved an old land surface beneath it, which molluscan and palynological evidence suggests had supported open grassland that had been cultivated at one time. The innermost circuit postdates numerous pits dug on the summit of the hill, most of which had been deliberately back-filled, frequently incorporating blocks of sarsen. Excavations by Dr Alasdair Whittle recovered an oval grave under the outer bank with post holes close by; the grave contained the crouched inhumation of a male about 35-40 years of age, who apparently had lain exposed in the grave before it was filled in. Charcoal from the old land surface beneath the outer bank produced a radiocarbon date of 2950 ± 150 bc, possibly relating to this pre-enclosure activity.

Dr Isobel Smith argued on the grounds of adjoining sherds of pottery from the three ditch circuits (all but one of which came from secondary ditch fills) that all three circuits were contemporary. However, sherds common to one vessel are frequently found in all three ditches stratified above one another, in some cases through the whole depth of the filling. This suggests that the chalk rubble of the ditch fills was radically disturbed (perhaps by re-cutting, which unless accompanied by massive organic deposition is virtually impossible to detect in chalk rubble) and that such widespread disturbance might have led to a few sherds being transmitted from one ditch circuit to another. The outer ditch is entirely different in stature (averaging 2.7 to 3 metres in depth) from the inner two circuits (with depth ranges of 0.7 to 1.9 metres), and its use probably persisted longer, with later neolithic and beaker pottery deposited within it — items rare within the inner two ditches. The question of cumulative or non-cumulative construction at Windmill Hill, however, remains unanswered.

The ditch stratigraphy at Windmill Hill is of considerable interest. It is in the deep outer ditch that the best record survives. Here, once again, there is no evidence of primary silting such as one might expect had the ditch been left open for even a full winter. Hard down on the native chalk are masses of angular blocks of chalk rubble, vacuous and sterile. It is tempting to suggest deliberate and assiduous cleaning before the catastrophic collapse of an unstable rampart. In this latter connection Smith, during her own control excavations on the site, located a row of post holes beneath the outer bank which may indicate the presence of a revetted forward face to this structure. Bulked charcoal from this layer (layer 4) yielded a radiocarbon date of 2570 ± 150 bc. This single date has often been viewed as rather late for a causewayed enclosure but, if regarded in its true context as a date for the final destruction of the site, then it may perhaps be accepted with less suspicion. This view may be reinforced by beaker pottery found in the top of the layer of compact chalky filling immediately overlying layer 4. The outer ditch produced relatively few finds, although recent work by Whittle has shown that deliberately placed spreads of animal bone occurred in the primary fill; at no stage has work on the outer circuit produced evidence of re-cutting.

The sequence in the middle circuit is initially similar to that described in the outer ditch. Again, there is little evidence of the 'sludgy' silting expected from an extended period of weathering. On the chalk floor of the ditch lies vacuous chalk rubble interdigitated with a few silty lenses and deposited 'bundles' of animal bone, pottery and flintwork, and organic staining also occurs on the ditch floor. Whittle's work demonstrates that such deposits occur throughout the primary and secondary filling and that a dug 'scoop' occurs in the top of the secondary silt filled with dark organic material. Much the same story is visible in the published sections of the inner ditch.

Leaving aside the issue of the contemporaneity of all three circuits at Windmill Hill, it is clear that the two inner circuits of the site can be equated with ceremonialised disposal of food debris and cultural material within ditches that were the subject initially of cleaning and then became subject to substantial blocks of filling moving rapidly from unstable banks.

The artefactual material from the site shows it was the focus of considerable wealth. Some 1300 individual pottery vessels are represented in the total assemblage as identified by Smith. Their fabrics show that there were four different sources for this pottery. Two must be relatively local. The other two, however, are from distant sources: one of gabbro ware from the Lizard peninsula in Cornwall, and the other the fabric gritted with oolitic limestone fragments from the area around Frome in Somerset. Pottery from this source also turns up in quantity at Hambledon

Hill, Robin Hood's Ball, Knap Hill and Whitesheet Hill.
A wide range of imported stone occurs on the site. In terms of grouped rocks alone material from Cornwall is present (Groups I, Ia and IIa — all Cornish south-coast resources suggesting that this site was participating in an exchange network distinct from and possibly at a later date than the Carn Brea — Helman Tor — Hembury — Maiden Castle — Hambledon connection). In addition, material came to the site from the axe quarries in Great Langdale, Cumbria (Group VI), Craig Lwyd (Group VII), the Prescelly Mountains in South Wales (Groups XIII and VIII) and a range of unidentified highland zone sources. Add to this a wide range of cherts, slates and sandstones and the emerging picture of wide-ranging contacts argues for an extraordinarily prestigious site, acting as a magnet attracting material from all over England and Wales.

The economy upon which this prestige was based is difficult to interpret. The site appears to be dominated by cattle bone, which in terms of the minimum number of individual animals present equals all other species put together. There is some evidence to suggest (as at Hambledon) the husbandry of these as much for their milk as for their flesh. Whereas (apart from red and roe deer antler, mostly cast) no wild-animal bone is found in pre-enclosure contexts (an admittedly small bone assemblage), deposits from within the ditches produced at least three individual foxes, four to six wild cattle, two hares, a badger, at least one wild cat and an unknown number of deer. Again, perhaps significantly in terms of the Hambledon evidence, whereas only three dog bones occur in pre-enclosure contents (in a bone assemblage approximately half the size of that from the ditches), 159 (21.9 per cent of the total assemblage) were located from the ditch deposits. Dennell, in an ingenious analysis of the grain impressions fired into pottery from the site, has shown the preference for the local pottery to exhibit barley impressions. Clearly Windmill Hill remained a centre of reverential regard (like Hambledon) for centuries, still persisting as a focus for activity to the end of the neolithic and beyond.

Briar Hill

The last site to consider, the enclosure at Briar Hill, Hardington, south-west of Northampton (SP 735594), is in a very different setting to Windmill Hill. It lies on a slight eminence on the north-facing slope of the Nene valley at a height about 75 to 80 metres OD. The site was excavated by Dr Helen Bamford between 1974 and 1978 and consisted of two closely spaced concentric circuits — the type that Palmer associates with the Midlands of England. Set within and probably superimposed upon this earlier two-circuit enclosure is a smaller oval-shaped enclosure set on a north-south axis. As at Windmill Hill, activity on the site clearly preceded the construction of any enclosure; furthermore, ceremonial functions continued on the site long after the enclosure's final abandonment.

The earliest activity on the site is represented by residual charcoals and a few possible structural features that have yielded early radiocarbon dates in the range 3730 ± 70 bc to 3490 ± 110 bc. Whether this activity is of neolithic origin or is associated with the late mesolithic microliths on the site (again in derived circumstances) is unknown. The first clearly defined neolithic activity on the site appears to be the construction of the outer and inner enclosure ditch circuit. The available evidence suggests that this activity took place before a range of carbon dates from organic material incorporated in the ditch filling — a range with a median date *c*.2600 ± 100 bc, setting this enclosure broadly contemporary with others in Britain, in the earlier centuries of the third millennium bc.

The remarkable feature of the initial enclosure at Briar Hill is the morphology of the filling pattern of the ditches. The multiplicity of re-cutting episodes present can be seen clearly. Frequently six or more quite independent phases of re-cutting are found within any one segment of the ditch. Unfortunately bone did not survive on the site, but organic and ashy staining at the base of many of the re-cuts may represent the kind of deposit which occurred on other sites. Pottery, predominantly of the Mildenhall style, from the ditch segments showed that material from one re-cutting phase became incorporated in a later phase and relatively little of it, or indeed of the flint assemblage (about 25 per cent), came from the double outer enclosure ditches. The bulk of the cultural material was deposited within the somewhat later 'inner spiral' or inner ovoid enclosure, which seems to have become the focus for a greater degree of depositional activity as time went by.

Of this inner ovoid enclosure no bank material survives *in situ* but Bamford was able to indicate, by virtue of the directional bias of the ditch filling, where the bank had stood. In the case of the outer two concentric ditch circuits, the bank stood, as we would expect with any typical causewayed enclosure, on the inner side of the ditch. However, where there is evidence for bank location in the case of the inner ovoid enclosure, it suggests that the bank stood *outside* the ditch. The inner ovoid is also of a geometrically precise form — an oval with its axis running due north-south, bisecting a 'screen' of (otherwise undated) post holes running tangentially to the enclosure on the north side.

All of these features are paralleled in henge monuments, the standard ceremonial enclosure type of the later third millennium and the later neolithic. Probably at a later stage in the life of the ovoid enclosure a rectilinear structure was built on the north-south axis of the enclosure. This structure was associated with grooved ware pottery (a late neolithic pottery style frequently associated with henge-monument construction) and produced a radiocarbon date of 2060 ± 90 bc. Bamford has misgivings about this interpretation of the site but the writer suggests that on this site, within the causewayed enclosure tradition, we can see the embryonic emergence and later fruition of the henge-monument tradition, as best exemplified by two other sites. One of them is Stonehenge itself, where the earliest phase of the monument's construction, extending back to the middle of the third millennium bc, comprised a severely circular *causewayed* ditch about 100 metres in diameter with, as if to emphasise its ancestry (and unique among henge monuments), its cognate bank on its *inner* side. The second site, a causewayed enclosure found in 1987 at Flagstones on the line of the Dorchester (Dorset) bypass, is severely circular in form and of about 100 metres projected diameter with low banks both in and outside the ditch. An antler pick from the ditch basal silts produced a radiocarbon date of 2130 ± 80 bc, firmly placing the monument in the late neolithic. Centrally located within it was a substantial round barrow overlying a single adult burial. Within the backfill of the grave pit was found *inter alia* a single copper-alloy rivet. The site appears to resemble the circular causewayed ditch mentioned above that surrounds the great later round barrow at Duggleby Howe in North Yorkshire.

In this book we have considered the origin of causewayed enclosures and the cultural and environmental milieu of which they were part. We have examined their role in the neolithic landscape and their function within neolithic society, observing how they reflect upon many aspects of earlier neolithic life. Finally, we have seen how this earlier form of enclosure in Britain contributes to the emergence of later neolithic and earlier bronze age architectural traditions, which are discussed in Shire Archaeology books on prehistoric henges (by Aubrey Burl, forthcoming) and barrows (by Leslie Grinsell; third edition, 1990).

6
Sites to visit

The sites suggested below are unrepresentative because they consist entirely of those hilltop enclosures that have survived the destructive hand of man. The majority of known causewayed enclosures (since 1970) — some 35 out of about fifty — are set on low spurs or knolls on, or overlooking, the flood plains of rivers. Not a single one of these sites has survived to a degree where any visit could be successfully directed or rewarding, other than to furnish an impression of location.

Barkhale, Bignor Hill, Madehurst, West Sussex. SU 976126. 13 km north-east of Chichester.

This large causewayed enclosure measures some 230 metres by 150 metres; there is a single circuit of ditch with an internal bank oval in shape. The earthworks of the site are best made out on the northern and north-eastern flanks.

Carn Brea, Illogan, Cornwall. SW 685407. 2 km south-west of Redruth.

The stone wall of the 1 ha eastern summit enclosure is still readily visible, as are some of the terraces that lie within it. The outer enclosure defences are also plainly visible, particularly on the south-eastern and southern flanks of the site. Finds from Carn Brea are displayed in the Cornwall County Museum, Truro.

Combe Hill, Jevington, East Sussex. TQ 574021. 3 km north-west of Eastbourne.

This is a small causewayed enclosure of about 0.6 ha. Two circuits of ditch exist on the site, of which the inner is plainly visible with a bank standing 0.5 metre high. The outer survives in the south-east and west sector. On the north side the ground is so steep that it is unlikely that any outer ditch was ever dug.

Crickley Hill, Coberley, Gloucestershire. SO 928161. 7.5 km south-south-west of Cheltenham.

Various aspects of the site are visible during the campaign of excavations and a visitor centre is planned. The site is a splendid location to visit.

Hambledon Hill, Iwerne Courtenay (or Shroton), Dorset. ST 849122. 8 km north-west of Blandford Forum.

At this site most of the earthworks have been totally reduced by cultivation. However, the west side of the main enclosure is preserved in permanent pasture and the causewayed ditch segments and bank are still visible. The excavated long barrow (restored) and southern cross-ditch of the enclosure are also visible at this location. The position and the northern bank scarp of the Stepleton enclosure is visible, as are the outwork ditches within the yew wood on the southern spur of the hill. The long barrow on the northern spur is a splendid monument while the keen fieldworker will soon locate the probably neolithic northern spur enclosure within the later iron age hillfort. Finds from Hambledon Hill are displayed in the Dorset County Museum, Dorchester.

Helman Tor, Lanlivery, Cornwall. SX 168607. 4.5 km west-north-west of Lostwithiel.

This is another beautiful hilltop setting in central Cornwall, very like Carn Brea to behold. The enclosure walls are visible, particularly on the east side of the site, as are some of the occupation terraces.

Hembury, Payhembury, Devon. ST 113031. 20 km north-east of Exeter.

This site is worth visiting if only to appreciate its situation. No visible surface traces of the neolithic causewayed enclosure exist, however. Finds from Hembury fort are displayed in the Royal Albert Memorial Museum, Exeter.

Knap Hill, Alton Priors, Wiltshire. SU 121636. 7.5 km south-west of Marlborough.

This is the most striking of all causewayed enclosures, when viewed from the Alton Priors to Marlborough road looking east. The ditch and bank surround three sides of a hillcrest enclosing an area of 2.4 ha. The segments of ditch and the cognate bank are clearly visible on the west side of the crest.

Robin Hood's Ball, Shrewton, Wiltshire. SU 103460. 7 km north-west of Amesbury.

This site is set within military ranges on Salisbury Plain and permission *must* (and may) be obtained from range wardens in order to visit the site.

Rybury Camp, All Cannings, Wiltshire. SU 083640. 10 km north-east of Devizes; 3 km west of Knap Hill (see above).

Traces of the neolithic camp can best be observed outside the later iron age hillfort rampart on the eastern slopes of the spur. The remains comprise a single arc of causewayed ditch (six segments) of an enclosure that may originally have enclosed some 2 ha. The possible remains of a further causewayed ditch, much damaged by chalk quarrying, can be seen 200 metres to the south on Cliffords Hill.

The Trundle, Singleton, West Sussex. SU 877110. 5 km north of Chichester.

The neolithic earthworks lie within the later iron age hillfort and the ditches and banks can just be seen on the ground. The remains comprise three circuits of ditch, an inner circuit about 120 metres in diameter, an outer circuit 305 metres in diameter, with an intermediate circuit which 'spirals' for 1¼ circuits between them.

Whitehawk Causewayed Enclosure, Kemp Town, Brighton, East Sussex. TQ 330048.

The site lies to either side of Manor Road at the southern end of the racecourse grandstands. Little remains to be seen of this site, which originally comprised four concentric rings of cause-wayed ditch covering a total of 7 ha. Today, of the four circuits of ditch, the third circuit from the centre is probably the most visible. About 90 metres north of Manor Road it leaves the racecourse (where it has been flattened) and makes its way to the south-east and can be seen as a quite distinct scarp along the very steep upper edge of Whitehawk Bottom.

Whitesheet Hill, Kilmington, Wiltshire. ST 802352. 12.5 km south-west of Warminster.

2 km north of the village of Mere in west Wiltshire, this site comprises a single circuit of causewayed ditch enclosing an area of 2.4 ha set upon a knoll on a spur protruding from the major massif of Whitesheet Hill.

Windmill Hill, Winterbourne Monkton, Wiltshire. SU 087714. 1.5 km north-west of Avebury.

The site is owned by the National Trust and is in the guardian-ship of English Heritage. It is set upon a very low eminence north-west of the great later neolithic ceremonial complex at

Avebury. Around the summit of the hill but slightly biased to the northern slope are set three concentric circuits of causewayed ditch. The total area enclosed is 9.6 ha. The innermost enclosure is about 85 metres in diameter and encloses 0.5 ha. The intermediate enclosure is about 200 metres in diameter, enclosing 3.15 ha. Finds from this site are displayed in Avebury Museum.

7
Further reading

General

Barker, G., and Webley, D. 'Causewayed Camps and Early Neolithic Economies in Central Southern England', *Proceedings of the Prehistoric Society*, XLIV (1978), 161-86.

Case, H. J. 'Neolithic Explanations', *Antiquity*, XLIII (1969), 176-86.

Curwen, E. C. 'Neolithic Camps', *Antiquity*, IV (1930), 22-54.

Dennell, R. W. 'Prehistoric Crop Cultivation in Southern England: A Reconsideration', *Antiquaries' Journal*, LVI (1976), 11-23.

Palmer, R. 'Interrupted Ditched Enclosures in Britain: The Use of Aerial Photography for Comparative Studies', *Proceedings of the Prehistoric Society*, XLII (1976), 161-86.

Piggott, S. *Neolithic Cultures of the British Isles*. Cambridge University Press, 1954.

Renfrew, A. C. 'Monuments, Mobilisation and Social Organisation in Neolithic Wessex' in A. C. Renfrew (editor), *The Explanation of Culture Change in Models in Prehistory*, 539-58. Duckworth, 1973.

Smith, I. F. 'Causewayed Enclosures', in D. D. A. Simpson (editor), *Economy and Settlement in Neolithic and Early Bronze Age Britain and Europe*, 89-112. Leicester University Press, 1971.

Smith, I. F. 'Windmill Hill and Its Implications', *Palaeohistoria*, XII (Groningen, 1966), 469-81.

Whittle, A. 'Earlier Neolithic Enclosures in Northwest Europe', *Proceedings of the Prehistoric Society*, XLIII (1977), 329-48.

Whittle, A. *The Earlier Neolithic of Southern England and Its Continental Background*. British Archaeological Reports, International Series, XXXV, Oxford, 1977.

Wilson, D. 'Causewayed Camps' and 'Interrupted Ditch Systems', *Antiquity*, XLIX (1975), 178-86.

Sites

Reference to some particularly full site reports are offered in alphabetical order.

Abingdon. Avery, M. 'The Neolithic Causewayed Enclosure, Abingdon', in H. J. Case and A. W. R. Whittle (editors),

Settlement Patterns in the Oxford Region, Council for British Archaeology Rescue Report, 44 (1982), 10-50. With references in bibliography.

Carn Brea. Mercer, R. J. 'Excavations at Carn Brea, Illogan, Cornwall 1970-73', *Cornish Archaeology*, XX (1981), 1-204.

Crickley Hill. Dixon, P. *Current Archaeology*, 76 (1981), 145-6. 'Crickley Hill' in Burgess, C. *et al* (editors). *Enclosures and Defences in the Neolithic of Western Europe*, British Archaeological Reports, International Series, 403 (1989).

Etton. Pryor, F. 'Etton, Maxey, Cambridgeshire' in Burgess, C., *et al* (editors). *Enclosures and Defences in the Neolithic of Western Europe*. British Archaeological Reports, International Series, 403 (1989).

Hambledon Hill. Mercer, R. J. *Hambledon Hill — A Neolithic Landscape*. Edinburgh University Press, 1980.

Staines. Robertson Mackay, R. 'The Neolithic Causewayed Enclosure at Staines, Surrey: Excavations 1961-3', *Proceedings of the Prehistoric Society*, LIII (1987), 23-128.

Windmill Hill. Smith, I. F. *Windmill Hill and Avebury — Excavations by Alexander Keiller 1925-39*. Cambridge University Press, 1965.

Index

Page numbers in italic refer to illustrations.